# SWIPE RIGHT ON LEADERSHIP

## NAVIGATING THE NEW RULES OF WORK WITH GEN Z

AKILAN A P

Made with ♥ on the Notion Press Platform
www.notionpress.com

To the dreamers and the doers, the pioneers of yesterday and the innovators of tomorrow, who remind us that leadership is not a position—it's a practice.

To Gen Z—you've brought energy, wit, and fearless authenticity to the workplace. Your ability to question norms, embrace change, and insist on purpose has challenged leaders to listen harder, lead better, and sometimes laugh at themselves. You teach us that leadership today is as much about adapting as it is about inspiring.

To the leaders forged in the fires of the Great Recession—your grit and perseverance built the foundation for resilience in the modern workplace. You've taught us that challenges, no matter how daunting, can be transformed into opportunities with vision and determination.

To every manager learning to bridge generational gaps, to every fresh hire wondering if they'll ever belong, and to every team navigating the glorious mess of hybrid schedules, Slack threads, and coffee-fueled brainstorms—this book is for you.

May we all find the courage to fail forward, the humility to learn from one another, and the audacity to build workplaces that thrive on trust, creativity, and collaboration.

Here's to the leaders we are and the ones we're becoming.

# Contents

# Contents

# Foreword

Leadership today looks nothing like it did twenty years ago, and that's not a bad thing. The workplace has shifted—no, evolved—into a dynamic space where generational diversity and technological advancements collide. In this chaos lies an incredible opportunity: to reimagine what it means to lead, collaborate, and thrive in a world that's constantly changing.

This book, Swipe Right on Leadership: Navigating the New Rules of Work with Gen Z, is a timely exploration of these shifts. It's not a dry leadership manual or a preachy "how-to" guide. Instead, it's a vivid, funny, and sometimes painfully honest story about a fresh-faced newcomer, Ethan, and a seasoned operations leader, Noah, learning to navigate not just the workplace but also each other.

Ethan represents the fearless, digital-native Gen Z—unapologetically authentic, skeptical of hierarchies, and determined to make an impact. Noah, on the other hand, is a leader forged during the Great Recession, a time when survival and efficiency were the name of the game. Their contrasting perspectives collide in a workplace that demands both innovation and precision.

What makes this book special is its relatability. It doesn't just tell you about leadership—it shows you. Through humorous missteps, awkward introductions, and unexpectedly profound moments, Ethan and Noah's journey reflects the realities of a workplace where everyone, regardless of generation, has something to teach and something to learn.

Whether you're a Gen Z professional figuring out your place in the corporate world, a seasoned leader grappling with new rules, or someone curious about how these two worlds interact, this book will make you laugh, think, and perhaps even rethink your own approach to leadership.

The stories here are more than fiction; they're a reflection of the new rules of work—a call to lead with empathy, adapt with courage, and grow together. Because at the end of the day, leadership isn't just about guiding others—it's about learning to lead ourselves.

Let Ethan and Noah take you on a journey through the glorious mess of hybrid schedules, Slack debates, TikTok captions, and coffee-fueled brainstorms. You'll see yourself in their struggles, and maybe even discover a new way to thrive in this ever-evolving workplace.

So, swipe right on this story—it's worth the match.

# Acknowledgements

To Gen Z—you've been the stars of this book and the delightful chaos of my professional life. For the late-night calls, the unfiltered feedback, and the way you roasted my every attempt to "relate," thank you. You've taught me that leadership today is as much about listening as it is about leading—and that sometimes, the best way to connect is to laugh at myself first.

To my team—you didn't just show up; you let me in. You shared your hopes, frustrations, and occasional brilliance, all while teaching me that true leadership comes from trust and openness. Even when you made me rethink my wardrobe choices or questioned why I still use punctuation in Slack messages, you made me better.

To my wife—your patience is the unsung hero of this book. From the late-night calls I couldn't ignore to the endless rants about generational gaps and emoji-driven feedback, you've listened, supported, and somehow managed to stay sane through it all. You've been my sounding board and my anchor, even when I didn't deserve it.

To the leaders who've trusted me—you've shown me what courage and humility look like in leadership. Whether it was embracing new ideas or pushing through the challenges of managing a multi-generational team, your resilience has been inspiring.

To my mentors—you've proven that leadership is a journey, not a destination. Your lessons, both spoken and unspoken, have shaped my perspective and kept me grounded (even when I wasn't).

And finally, to the workplace itself—the glorious mess of hybrid schedules, Slack debates, and coffee-fueled brainstorms. You've been my testing ground and my teacher. This book exists because of the lessons, the laughter, and yes, the roasts.

Here's to the late-night calls, the team who made it all worth it, and the moments that turned into stories.

Cheers!

## CHAPTER I

# Welcome to SynergyWorks

Ethan adjusted his tie for the fourth time that morning, staring at his reflection with growing doubt. The starched white shirt clung to his chest uncomfortably, its sharp creases like little reminders of the pressure to impress. "First impressions matter," his mom had drilled into him over breakfast, sliding a perfectly ironed shirt his way. "It's a tech company, Mom," he'd argued. "People probably show up in hoodies." Her response? A raised eyebrow and the unrelenting delivery of the shirt, tie, and polished shoes.

Now, here he was, in front of the mirror, feeling like an overdressed penguin about to waddle into a rave. *Seriously, Mom? A tie? At a tech company? It's like she thinks I'm interviewing for CEO, not a junior operations role.* He sighed, giving the tie one last, futile tug. *Maybe I should just ditch the jacket altogether. Nah, that'd probably make me look even more awkward.*

His phone buzzed on the dresser, the screen lighting up with a text from his best friend, Mark. Good luck, corporate bro. Don't let them eat you alive. Let me know if you need a rescue squad.

Ethan grinned, typing back: Noted. SOS signal is polished shoes and tears.

SynergyWorks' headquarters was impossible to miss—a gleaming tower of glass and steel that dominated the city's skyline. As Ethan approached, he couldn't help but gawk. Everything about the building screamed innovation, from the angular design to the holographic logo spinning above the entrance. *Okay, they're definitely not subtle about this "innovation" thing.* He wondered if the holographic logo was powered by some cutting-edge technology or if it was just a fancy light show. *Probably the latter*, he thought cynically.

He paused at the doors, catching his reflection. His mom's voice echoed in his mind again, but this time, it mingled with his own nagging doubt. The outfit might have worked for a high-stakes banking firm, but here? He looked like someone's overly earnest prom date. Behind him, a trio of employees breezed by, laughing and chatting. One wore joggers, another carried a skateboard, and the third had a hoodie so oversized it might have doubled as a blanket.

Ethan pulled at his cuffs. *I'm going to stick out like a LinkedIn post surrounded by TikToks.* He imagined trying to explain the concept of "business casual" to his mom. *She'd probably tell me to wear a suit made of khakis.*

The lobby was a shrine to modern corporate cool. Sharp lines and glowing accents created an atmosphere that felt both futuristic and intimidating. Digital screens displayed SynergyWorks' achievements on a continuous loop: "Most Innovative SaaS Solution of the Year," "Top 50 Tech Companies to Work For," and "Employee-Centric Workplace Award, 2023."

Ethan squinted at the smiling faces flashing across the screens, each employee mid-laugh or mid-brainstorm. They looked like they'd been plucked from a stock photo shoot. Right. *Employee-centric. Sure. Bet they bribed these people with free kombucha.* He wondered if the kombucha was on tap or if you had to fill out a form to get a cup.

At the reception desk, a cheerful assistant with perfectly manicured nails handed Ethan a visitor badge and directed him to the second floor. As he stepped into the elevator, a group of employees joined him—one balancing an iced coffee precariously on their laptop, another muttering into an AirPod about "last-minute sprints." Ethan's reflection stared back at him from the elevator's mirrored walls, a glaring reminder of how overdressed he was. *Note to self: Invest in some stylish sneakers. And maybe a hoodie.*

The elevator doors slid open, revealing a hive of activity. The second floor was an open workspace flooded with natural light, thanks to floor-to-ceiling windows. Rows of standing desks buzzed with activity, collaboration pods hummed with conversations, and neon notes covered whiteboards like the aftermath of a brainstorming tornado. Ethan spotted one that read, "Move Fast, Break Everything." Next to it, another proclaimed, "Innovate. Accelerate. Dominate."

Ethan stopped, half-horrified, half-amused. "Okay, poster. Relax," he muttered under his breath.

"Don't worry, they're just for show," someone said behind him. He turned to see a woman with cropped pink hair, dressed in sneakers and ripped jeans. She smirked. "But if you stare too long, you might get indoctrinated."

Ethan chuckled nervously. "Noted." He wondered if there was a secret handshake or a required chant to fully embrace the SynergyWorks culture.

The orientation room was already half-full when Ethan arrived. He slipped into a seat at the back, clutching his visitor folder like a life raft. At the front of the room, a man in a navy polo—Michael from HR, judging by his name tag—was arranging a set of glossy folders and beaming with the kind of energy Ethan could only describe as "caffeinated optimism." *This guy's either genuinely enthusiastic or he's had way too much coffee*, Ethan thought.

"Good morning, everyone!" Michael called, his voice booming. "Welcome to SynergyWorks! You're officially part of the best of the best!"

Ethan glanced at the woman next to him, who looked as skeptical as he felt. "Does he always talk like that?" Ethan whispered.

She smirked, hiding her laugh behind her hand. "I think he has a second job as a motivational speaker."

Michael launched into a slide deck titled "From Garage to Greatness." The presentation was a whirlwind of corporate buzzwords—synergy, scalability, disruption. Ethan tried to focus, but his gaze kept wandering to the bowl of mints on the table. *How many can I grab before it gets weird?* He made a mental note to calculate the optimal mint-to-buzzword ratio.

Noah Collins walked in halfway through the presentation, and the atmosphere in the room shifted immediately. Dark chinos, a crisp button-down, and the kind of confident stride that could part seas. Noah wasn't loud, but his presence spoke volumes. He took his place at the front of the room with a practiced ease, his sharp eyes scanning the new hires.

"I am Noah, the Head of Operations. This is a place for hard work, accountability, and results," Noah said, his voice even but firm. "If you thrive on delivering value, you'll fit in. If not, this might not be the place for you."

Ethan leaned forward slightly, studying him, *my boss*, he thought. *Motivational or subtly threatening? Jury's still out*. He wondered if Noah had a secret formula for success or if he just naturally exuded an aura of power.

Noah's gaze swept the room, pausing briefly on Ethan. For a moment, it felt like a spotlight had been trained on him. Ethan straightened in his chair, giving a small, uncertain nod. Noah moved on without acknowledgment, but Ethan felt like he'd just been entered into some unspoken evaluation. *Okay, Noah. Challenge accepted,* Ethan thought.

By lunch, Ethan's stomach was growling louder than his nerves. He followed Sophie—bubbly and effortlessly confident—and Amir, whose quiet, calm demeanor was a stark contrast to Ethan's jittery energy, to the cafeteria. The space was predictably Instagram-worthy: hanging plants, sleek furniture, and a kombucha station that practically glowed. *Seriously, they have a kombucha station. I'm starting to think this place is sponsored by Whole Foods*, Ethan mused.

Ethan, however, made a beeline for the fries and soda. *Forget green smoothies. I'm surviving on the greasy, sugary fuel of french fries and soda today*. He grabbed a handful of napkins, just in case.

"So," Sophie asked, biting into her salad, "first impressions?"

Ethan shrugged, dipping a fry into ketchup. "HR guy's too peppy. Noah Collins? Feels like he irons his shoelaces."

Amir chuckled. "He's probably the type to email you at 4 a.m. and expect a reply by 4:01."

Ethan grinned. "Exactly. Can't wait to see how that goes." He imagined setting up an auto-reply for emails received between midnight and 6 a.m.: "Gone fishin'. Or, you know, sleeping."

They were interrupted by a conversation at the next table. A couple of employees were discussing a recent project, throwing around terms like "agile development" and "sprint cycles." Ethan felt a pang of inadequacy. *I understood maybe half of those words,* he thought.

The afternoon session featured team introductions. Each newbie stood to share their name, role, and a surprising fact. Ethan's turn came last.

"Hi, I'm Ethan," he began, his voice a little hesitant but carrying a hint of humor. "Part of the operations team. And, uh... I once went viral on TikTok for accidentally spilling coffee on my dog during a livestream. Don't worry, she's fine—and a star now."

The room broke into a mix of chuckles and raised eyebrows. Sophie laughed out loud, nearly choking on her sip of water. "No way—you're that guy? The one with the golden retriever and the 'oops' coffee moment?"

Ethan nodded sheepishly. "That's me. Luna got more sponsorship offers than I ever will."

Even Noah smirked, though he quickly masked it by glancing down at his notes. Ethan caught the subtle reaction, feeling a small victory bloom in his chest. For a moment, the tension in the room lifted, and he felt a little more human—less "fresh meat."

The room erupted into laughter, and Ethan relaxed slightly, relieved to see even Noah crack a smile—just a little. Maybe there's hope for me yet, he thought.

As the day wound down, Ethan found himself lingering in the lobby with Sophie and Amir. "You coming to the mixer?" Sophie asked, scrolling through her phone.

"Mixer?" Ethan echoed.

"Yeah," Amir said. "Apparently it's a thing here. Free drinks. Also, more kombucha."

Ethan hesitated. Networking sounded exhausting. Free drinks sounded...less exhausting. Plus, I could use a drink after this day, he thought.

"I'll think about it," he said.

The mixer was in full swing when Ethan arrived, string lights twinkling overhead and upbeat music humming in the background. He stuck close to Sophie and Amir, laughing at Sophie's stories and listening to Amir's quiet insights. He even managed to strike up a conversation with a couple of other new hires, bonding over their shared confusion about "cross-functional permissions" and the sheer number of Slack channels they'd been added to.

Sophie teasingly asks, "So, where's Luna now? Signing autographs?"

Ethan replies, "Pretty much. I think she's angling for her own brand of dog-friendly coffee."

Amir, previously quiet, adds dryly, "At least one of you is successful on social media."

By the end of the evening, Ethan felt a surprising sense of belonging. The day had been a whirlwind, but for the first time, he started to believe that SynergyWorks might be more than just a job—it might be the beginning of something bigger. Or maybe it's just the free drinks talking, he thought.

*Okay, so maybe sharing my TikTok fame wasn't the best move, but at least it got a laugh. And hey, if I survived Noah Collins' smirk without combusting, maybe I'll make it through this job after all.* He glanced over at Noah, who was deep in conversation with a group of senior managers. Or maybe I'll just get fired for accidentally liking his ex-girlfriend's Instagram post from three years ago. The possibilities are endless.

Ethan left the mixer with a buzz in his head, a mix of exhaustion, excitement, and a healthy dose of apprehension. He wasn't sure what the future held at SynergyWorks, but he was ready to face it head-on. Or at least with a good supply of coffee and french fries, he thought.

CHAPTER II

# Settling In

**Morning Energy**

The office was alive when Ethan arrived. Employees darted from desk to desk, coffee cups in hand and laptops balanced precariously. Conversations overlapped, creating a hum of activity. It was almost energizing—almost. *More like organized chaos*, Ethan thought, navigating the crowded workspace. He bumped into someone rushing by, spilling a bit of their coffee. “Sorry!” he mumbled, feeling a flush of anxiety.

Sophie waved him over to her desk. “Morning, corporate bro,” she said with a grin. “Day two. You survived the first hurdle.”

Ethan smirked, plopping down in the chair beside her. “Barely. What’s next, running the gauntlet?”

She chuckled. “Pretty much. Just wait till the department tours. They’ll throw so much at you, your brain’ll need a hard reset.”

Amir, standing nearby, added quietly, “I’ve heard the Operations department can be...intense.” He’d worked in a similar structured environment before, and the subtle tension he sensed reminded him of it.

“Intense how?” Ethan asked, a flicker of unease in his stomach.

Amir shrugged slightly. “Just...organized. Very by-the-book.” He didn’t want to overstate it, especially on Ethan’s second day.

“Awesome,” Ethan muttered, already feeling the weight of the day ahead. *Great. Just what I needed.*

**Laptop Distribution and Tools Training**

The newbies gathered in a conference room that could comfortably fit twenty but had been crammed with thirty. Stacks of branded laptops sat on the table, each with a sticky note bearing a name. Ethan found his, the pristine device gleaming under the fluorescent lights. *My precious*, he thought, *half-jokingly, half-seriously.*

Michael bounced into the room with his usual enthusiasm. “Alright, team! Time to get you set up with everything you need to be the best of the best!”

Ethan caught Sophie rolling her eyes and stifled a laugh. *Someone needs to tell this guy that "best of the best" is so 2010.*

For the next hour, they fumbled through setting up their accounts. Michael's instructions, peppered with corporate jargon like "seamless integration" and "synergizing workflows," did little to ease the frustration. *Synergizing workflows? Is that even a verb?* Ethan thought, his fingers flying across the keyboard in a desperate attempt to keep up.

"Okay, so for the Productivity Suite, you'll want to enable cross-functional permissions," Michael announced, pointing to a convoluted set of steps on the screen.

"What does that even mean?" Ethan whispered to Amir, who shrugged in response. He was just as lost as Ethan.

Eventually, they moved on to a session introducing the company's internal communication tools. A tech support specialist named Craig took over, walking them through everything from Slack channels to project management dashboards.

"You'll spend 90% of your time here," Craig joked, pointing to a channel labeled #general. "And the other 10% arguing about deadlines in private threads."

Ethan followed along, but his attention wandered to the sheer volume of tools. Each seemed designed to solve a problem he hadn't known existed. *Do we really need five different apps just to communicate with each other? he wondered.*

"Is it just me," he muttered to Sophie, "or does it feel like they're training us to use tools instead of doing actual work?"

"It's not just you," she replied, hiding a grin. "It's called 'efficiency.'"

**The Tours Begin: Marketing**

"First stop: Marketing," Michael announced, his tone like a game show host.

Ethan's skepticism melted as they stepped into the Marketing department. It was like entering a parallel universe. The walls were lined with vibrant mood boards and half-finished campaign sketches. Jessica, the team lead, greeted them with the kind of warm energy that immediately put people at ease.

"This," she said, gesturing to the bustling room, "is where the magic happens. Campaigns, branding, messaging—it all starts here."

She led them to a cluster of desks where a small group was huddled around a laptop, debating color palettes for an ad. Jessica smiled. "We brainstorm, we argue, and eventually, we create something amazing. Creativity's the heartbeat of this department."

Ethan watched as she flipped through a presentation on her screen. It was a series of sleek, visually stunning slides showcasing a recent campaign.

"Wow," Ethan muttered, unable to hide his admiration.

Jessica caught his expression and grinned. "It's fun, but it's not all chaos. Once the ideas are there, we polish until they shine."

Ethan found himself nodding along. The energy, the collaboration, the tangible creativity—it felt alive in a way Operations hadn't. He could imagine himself here, bouncing ideas around, contributing to something vibrant. *Maybe I should have majored in marketing, he thought, a flicker of regret mixing with his fascination.*

**Next Stop: Product Development**

If Marketing was a whirlwind of creativity, Product Development was its logical counterpoint. The department had an almost Zen-like atmosphere—clean desks, carefully organized tools, and a palpable sense of focus.

Arjun, a quiet, methodical engineer, walked them through the space. "In Product, precision is everything," he explained, showing off a prototype on his laptop. "Every feature we create is tested, retested, and refined. The goal is seamless user experience."

Ethan was fascinated as Arjun demonstrated how tiny tweaks in a feature could drastically improve functionality. The quiet intensity of the work appealed to him in a different way than Marketing. Here, there was a clear purpose, a sense of craftsmanship. *It's like building with Legos, but for grown-ups*, Ethan thought.

"What I love most," Arjun continued, "is seeing an idea go from a rough sketch to something real, something people can use."

Ethan couldn't help but think, *This makes sense. I could see myself building something here, solving problems, making things better.*

**Operations Reality Check**

But then, there was Operations.

The stark, orderly space reminded Ethan of a library where noise was strictly forbidden. Spreadsheets filled screens, desks were aligned with military precision, and the air felt heavier somehow. *It's like stepping into a spreadsheet factory,* Ethan thought.

Noah stood at the front of the room, addressing the group with his usual commanding presence. "Operations is the backbone of this company," he began, his voice crisp. "Without structure, there's no foundation. Without precision, there's no success."

Ethan tried to focus, but his thoughts wandered back to Jessica's mood boards and Arjun's prototypes. Operations felt like a machine—necessary but devoid of the spark he'd seen in the other departments. *More like a well-oiled, soul-crushing machine,* he amended in his thoughts.

Noah continued, "Processes aren't negotiable. They ensure quality and efficiency. If you think you can shortcut your way through this, you'll find yourself correcting a lot of costly mistakes."

Ethan swallowed hard, feeling Noah's words directed at him even though they weren't. *Great,* he thought. *Exactly what I needed to hear after an already overwhelming day.* He wondered if Noah ever smiled, or if his face was permanently set in "intimidating mode." He noticed that even some of the more experienced-looking employees seemed a little more subdued in Noah's presence.

**Lunch Break: Conversations**

By lunchtime, Ethan's head was spinning. He joined Sophie and Amir in the cafeteria, seeking solace in a plate of fries and a soda. *The only constants in this universe are death, taxes, and the deliciousness of french fries,* he thought.

"So, what do you think of the tours?" Sophie asked, popping a piece of lettuce into her mouth.

Ethan sighed. "Marketing and Product were amazing. I could see myself fitting in there, you know? But Operations? It's like stepping into a factory. Everything's so...rigid."

Amir nodded. "It's an adjustment, for sure. Every company has its own rhythm, I guess."

Ethan frowned, poking at his fries. "Yeah, but how do you even breathe in an environment like that? It's all rules and no room for ideas."

Sophie smiled. "You'll figure it out. Maybe you're just more of a Marketing guy stuck in Operations."

Ethan chuckled. "That's what it feels like. Why didn't I apply there instead?" He wondered if it was too late to switch departments.

**Workshops and Icebreakers**

After lunch, the newbies reconvened in the main conference room for what Michael called "Interactive Team Integration." Ethan didn't need a translator to know it was corporate-speak for icebreakers. *Prepare for awkwardness,* he thought.

The first activity was a simple "two truths and a lie" game. Ethan was mildly impressed by some of his colleagues' creativity—one claimed to have wrestled an alligator (*and even had a blurry and even had a blurry photo on their phone to 'prove' it*), while another insisted they'd invented their own cryptocurrency (which, upon further questioning, turned out to be a Ponzi scheme involving digital tulips). Ethan wondered *if lying was a prerequisite for working at SynergyWorks.*

When it was Ethan's turn, he hesitated for a moment before speaking. "Alright. I've never broken a bone, I once went viral on TikTok, and I hate coffee."

"TikTok is definitely true," Sophie piped up immediately. "You mentioned it yesterday."

"Yeah, but who hates coffee?" Amir asked skeptically.

Ethan grinned. "You're right—it's the coffee. Can't live without it." He'd almost gone with "I can speak fluent Klingon," but decided that might be a bit too weird for day two.

The room chuckled, and for the first time that day, Ethan felt like he wasn't entirely out of place. *Maybe these people aren't so bad after all,* he thought.

**Interactive Tools Demo**

The second workshop of the afternoon involved navigating a mock project using the company's proprietary software. Ethan's group was tasked with creating a fictional proposal for a client.

"Think of it as practice for collaboration," Michael explained, handing out instructions. *Or practice for tearing your hair out in frustration*, Ethan thought.

The software, while sleek, was intimidating. Ethan's group spent the first ten minutes fumbling with permissions and sharing files before they could even start brainstorming. The interface was a labyrinth of drop-down menus and cryptic icons. Ethan accidentally clicked on something labeled "Quantum Entanglement Protocol" and his screen briefly displayed a picture of a cat riding a unicorn.

"I thought this was supposed to make things easier," Ethan muttered, his frustration rising.

"Welcome to corporate life," Sophie quipped, clicking furiously at her screen. She'd somehow managed to navigate to a page that appeared to be entirely in Wingdings.

Despite the initial chaos, the group eventually found their rhythm. Amir, who seemed to have a knack for organization, took the lead in structuring their proposal. Sophie threw in bold ideas that made the concept pop, and

Ethan, determined to contribute, suggested a few tweaks to streamline their presentation. He even managed to decipher a few of the cryptic icons, a small victory in the face of overwhelming technological adversity.

By the end of the session, their group had produced something halfway decent. Michael clapped enthusiastically as each team presented their mock proposals, offering generic praise like, “Great synergy!” and “Innovative thinking!” *Translation: "You didn’t completely crash the system, so good job!"* Ethan thought.

Ethan couldn’t decide whether to feel accomplished or patronized. He glanced over at Noah, who was observing the presentations with his usual unreadable expression. Probably the latter, he concluded.

**End-of-Day Reflections**

By the time the day wound down, Ethan’s brain felt like it had run a marathon. His laptop was loaded with tools he barely understood, and his head buzzed with instructions he’d probably forget by morning. *I‘m going to need a flowchart just to remember how to log in tomorrow,* he thought.

He returned to his desk, sinking into his chair with a sigh. Across the room, Noah was speaking with another manager, his arms crossed and expression as unreadable as ever. Even from a distance, he radiated an aura of quiet intensity. Ethan wondered what they were discussing. Probably something incredibly important and strategic. *Or maybe they’re just trying to figure out how to get the coffee machine to work.*

Sophie and Amir swung by as he was packing up.

“Dinner?” Sophie asked, her tone light.

Ethan hesitated. Part of him wanted to collapse on his couch and zone out, but the idea of being alone with his thoughts didn’t feel appealing either. *Plus, I need to debrief this day with someone who understands the sheer terror of "cross-functional permissions,"* he thought.

“Sure,” he said, slinging his bag over his shoulder.

**Dinner Conversations**

The trio found themselves at a cozy diner down the street, the kind of place where the coffee was always hot and the fries were perfectly crispy. Over burgers and milkshakes, they debriefed the day.

“Okay,” Sophie said, leaning forward. “Be honest—how overwhelmed are you right now?”

Ethan laughed. “On a scale of one to ten? About a twelve.”

Amir nodded in agreement. “There’s a lot to take in, but it gets easier. Once you start working on real projects, things click into place.”

“Does Noah ever, you know...ease up?” Ethan asked cautiously.

Sophie and Amir exchanged a look.

“He’s demanding,” Sophie said. “But I’ve heard he respects hard work. And he’s not unreasonable.”

Amir added, “He pushes people, but he also pushes for them to succeed. I think he genuinely wants his team to do well.”

Ethan wasn’t sure if that was reassuring or terrifying, but he appreciated their honesty. *So, basically, he’s a benevolent dictator?* he thought.

**Closing the Day**

Later that night, Ethan sprawled on his couch, staring at the ceiling. His thoughts wandered to the day’s events—the overwhelming number of tools, the forced icebreakers, and the looming specter of Noah’s expectations. *Maybe I should just quit and become a professional dog walker,* he thought, only half-joking.

Part of him felt drained, but another part felt a flicker of determination. It wasn’t the kind of day he’d dreamed of when he’d taken the job, but it was a start. And for now, that was enough. He thought about the vibrant energy of the Marketing department, the quiet focus of Product Development. He thought about the challenge Noah presented, the opportunity to prove himself. *Okay, maybe I won’t quit just yet, he thought. But if they make me do another icebreaker tomorrow, I’m out.*

CHAPTER III

# Meeting the Team

Ethan's confidence was a carefully constructed facade on Day Three at SynergyWorks. He strode into the office, dark chinos, polo shirt, and meticulously chosen sneakers projecting an air of casual coolness. He gave a passing colleague a nod that was half-acknowledgment, half-defiance. Relaxed tech guy? Nailed it. But beneath the surface, a knot of anxiety tightened in his stomach.

Michael, perched at reception as always, greeted Ethan with a grin so wide it could rival the Cheshire Cat's. His coffee mug – boldly emblazoned with "Think. Build. Scale." – completed the image of unbridled corporate enthusiasm. *Ethan wondered if Michael slept with the mug, or if he had a whole collection for different days of the week.*

"Morning, Ethan! Ready for Round Three?" Michael's voice was like a shot of espresso, pure caffeine-fueled cheer.

"Absolutely," Ethan replied, adjusting his messenger bag and trying to match Michael's energy, though his smile felt a bit like a strained grimace. "And I think I've finally nailed the 'business casual tech guy' look."

Michael chuckled, seemingly oblivious to Ethan's forced enthusiasm. "You're catching on. Here's the plan: spend the morning with your team. Noah's leading their weekly sync. After lunch, we'll pick up with orientation."

Ethan nodded, the knot in his stomach tightening. "Weekly sync, got it." *Sounds thrilling, he thought. Maybe they'll have a PowerPoint presentation with animated graphs.*

Michael leaned in slightly, his tone dropping as if imparting ancient wisdom. "Heads up: Noah's... intense. Don't take it personally."

"Great," Ethan muttered under his breath. "*Just what I needed – intensity before coffee.*" He imagined Noah as a corporate superhero, his superpower being the ability to induce anxiety with a single glance.

**Settling In**

At his desk, Ethan found his minimalist setup waiting for him: a sleek monitor, ergonomic chair, and a desk plant that looked like it had survived the Great Depression and emerged stronger. *Maybe it's Noah's secret weapon, Ethan thought. He uses it to test the resilience of new hires, like Louis*

*Litt from Suits*. Unfortunately, the plant was also in full view of Noah's desk, practically a spotlight for potential judgment.

Michael's cheerful voice snapped Ethan out of his thoughts. "Oh, and you'll be introducing yourself during the meeting."

Ethan froze mid-adjustment of his chair. "Wait, that's, like, on the agenda?"

Michael pointed at the meeting invite on Ethan's calendar, where the words "New Team Member Introduction: Ethan" stared back at him like a bad Tinder bio.

"Yep!" Michael chirped. "You'll do great!" He bounced away, leaving Ethan to grapple with the impending doom of public speaking.

Who decided introductions need to be impactful in two sentences? Ethan wondered. I mean, *who's impactful in two sentences? A Marvel character?* Maybe I should introduce myself as 'Ethan, aka The Internator, here to terminate inefficiency and optimize workflows.' He cringed. No, that's even worse.

**Practice Makes (Im)Perfect**

Ethan spent the next twenty minutes rehearsing, his desk a stage and his pen a reluctant microphone.

"Hi, everyone. I'm Ethan, and I'm super excited to join SynergyWorks!" He grimaced. Too basic. They'll smell the panic on me.

He tried again, adopting a more casual tone. "Yo, what's up? I'm Ethan. Fresh grad, big ideas, ready to crush it in Ops—"

He winced. *Crush it? Did I time-travel to 2015?*

Lowering his voice, he gave it one last shot. "Hi, I'm Ethan. Just happy to be here and ready to hit the ground running." *Ugh, that sounds like something out of a corporate brochure.*

The sound of someone clearing their throat made Ethan jump. Zara, the team's resource coordinator, stood nearby, smirking as she handed him a stack of documents. "Relax," she said. "They don't bite. Much."

Ethan laughed nervously. *She says they don't bite, but I'm convinced Noah's critiques come with a side of fangs*. He wondered if Zara had any survival tips for navigating Noah's intensity.

**The Weekly Sync**

Conference Room B buzzed with quiet energy as Ethan slid into a seat near the back. Laptops were open, coffee mugs decorated the table, and cryptic slogans – "Work Smart. Play Harder." – peppered the room. Ethan wondered if there was a secret decoder ring for understanding

SynergyWorks' corporate lingo.

At exactly 10:00 AM, Noah strode in, exuding a calm authority that immediately commanded attention. The room settled like a classroom on the verge of a pop quiz. Ethan felt a bead of sweat trickle down his temple.

"Morning," Noah said briskly. He opened his laptop, displaying a slide deck with stark, no-frills text. *No fancy animations? Disappointing,* Ethan thought. "We have a lot to get through. Let's begin."

What followed was 45 minutes of critiques and directives delivered with the precision of a military strategist. Noah's tone was steady, but his words carried the weight of a gavel.

"You missed a deadline," he told one team member, his voice devoid of emotion. "What's your plan to ensure this doesn't happen again?"

The team member stammered, "I, uh—"

"No excuses. I need solutions."

Ethan gripped his pen tightly. *Ever feel like you're an extra in a movie you didn't audition for? Yeah, that was me. And the movie was Noah Collins: Deadline Enforcer.* He wondered if Noah had a secret lair where he practiced his intimidating glares.

**The Introduction**

"Finally," Noah said, glancing at his smartwatch, "we have a new team member. Ethan, introduce yourself."

Every head turned. Ethan felt his stomach somersault as he stood. His carefully rehearsed lines evaporated, leaving him with nothing but sheer panic and improv instincts.

"Yo, what's up, team? I'm Ethan," he began, his voice teetering between confidence and desperation. "Fresh grad, ready to bring good vibes and big ideas to Ops. If you need me, just ping me on Slack or, you know, slide into my DMs – no cap."

The room froze. Someone coughed. Zara bit her lip to stifle a laugh.

Noah's expression didn't shift, but his jaw tensed. *He's about to vaporize me with his mind,* Ethan thought.

"Thank you, Ethan. Enthusiasm is noted. In the future, let's prioritize clarity and professionalism."

*Translation: don't talk like Twitter*, Ethan muttered under his breath as he sat back down. Lesson learned.

**A Change in Plans**

As the meeting ended, Ethan began gathering his things, eager to slink away unnoticed. But Noah motioned for him to stay.

"Ethan, a minute?"

"Sure," Ethan said, his voice a half-octave higher than usual. He sat back down, clutching his notebook like a shield.

Once the room cleared, Noah leaned against the table, arms crossed. "Operations isn't about charm or improvisation," he said. "It's about results."

Ethan nodded quickly. "Absolutely. Results. Totally my thing." *Please don't fire me,* he added silently.

Noah didn't react. "For today, you'll shadow Megan. She'll walk you through workflows."

Ethan hesitated. "I thought I had orientation sessions this afternoon—"

"Are you on Michael's team or mine?" Noah's tone remained calm, but the words were sharp.

"Yours," Ethan replied, swallowing hard.

"Good. Then your priority is here. Understand the work, and don't just follow instructions – ask why we do things a certain way."

Ethan nodded. "Got it. Focus on the work. I'll make it happen." *And try not to say anything stupid.*

Noah's gaze softened – just barely. "Be sharp. Pay attention. And leave the DMs for social media."

Ethan stood, fumbling slightly with his notebook. "Thanks for the clarity," he said, cringing internally. *Note to self: don't try to sound profound. It just makes things worse.*

As he left the room, Ethan exhaled sharply. *Day three motto: stay sharp, ask why, and maybe delete 'no cap' from my vocabulary forever.*

**Lunch Break: Sharing War Stories**

By the time lunch rolled around, Ethan felt like he'd run a mental marathon. He made his way to the café, eager for a break and maybe some moral support. The space was bustling with employees juggling salads, sandwiches, and enough coffee to power a small country. Ethan wondered if they had a caffeine IV drip station somewhere.

He spotted Sophie and Amir at a corner table and waved as he approached. Sophie greeted him with her usual bubbly grin, while Amir nodded, his mouth full of what looked like a very questionable wrap.

"Please tell me someone else had a terrifying morning," Ethan said, collapsing into a chair.

"Define 'terrifying,'" Sophie replied, stirring her green smoothie. "Because I almost cried trying to configure my Slack notifications."

Ethan raised an eyebrow. "Pretty sure I take the cake. I had to introduce myself in Noah's weekly sync."

Amir stopped mid-chew, his eyes widening. "You spoke? In front of Noah? On purpose?"

"Not on purpose!" Ethan groaned. "It was on the agenda. I tried to keep it simple, but somehow I ended up saying 'slide into my DMs.'"

Sophie burst out laughing, nearly spilling her smoothie. "You did not."

"I did," Ethan said, burying his face in his hands. "He told me to focus on clarity and professionalism. Which is corporate speak for 'never say that again.'"

Amir shook his head. "Man, Noah's intense. I saw him yesterday near the elevators, and I swear he gave me a look that said, 'Be productive or perish.'"

"Exactly!" Ethan said, sitting up. "It's like he doesn't have to yell. His disappointment is loud enough on its own."

Sophie nodded. "Oh, totally. I saw him in a meeting with my manager, and he didn't even have to speak. Just tapped his watch and raised an eyebrow. The whole room went silent."

Ethan leaned back, his gaze drifting to the café's kombucha station. A group of employees were huddled around it, discussing the different flavors with the kind of seriousness usually reserved for wine tastings. *Is this what adulthood is? Ethan wondered. Trying to figure out tools you've never heard of while avoiding a manager who could vaporize you with one look and deciphering the complex world of kombucha?*

"So, is this what adulthood is?" he asked aloud. "Trying to figure out tools you've never heard of while avoiding a manager who could vaporize you with one look?"

"Basically," Amir replied, unwrapping a cookie. "But at least we get cookies. That's something."

Ethan laughed, feeling a bit lighter. "True. And honestly, if Noah's the scariest thing here, maybe I'll survive after all."

Sophie raised her smoothie like a toast. "To survival. Day Three and counting."

Ethan clinked his water bottle against it. "Day Three. No more 'DMs' and no cap."

Amir smirked. "What's 'no cap' mean anyway?"

Ethan froze, then sighed. "It means 'seriously.' And yes, I see the irony. Let's pretend this conversation never happened."

The group dissolved into laughter, and for the first time all day, Ethan felt like he might be okay. He still had a lot to learn, a lot of challenges to face, but he was starting to realize that maybe, just maybe, he could navigate this strange new world of corporate life. And maybe, just maybe, he could even find a way to make it his own.

CHAPTER IV

# Meeting Megan

Ethan shuffled towards Megan's desk, his body language a symphony of awkwardness. He fidgeted with the strap of his messenger bag, his gaze darting around the office like a startled hummingbird. The notebook in his hand was clutched so tightly his knuckles were turning white. Around him, the office buzzed with the chaotic symphony of corporate life—keyboards clacking in an almost aggressive rhythm, phones ringing intermittently, and the low murmur of people debating deadlines over the hum of overworked AC units. The air carried a faint smell of stale coffee and desperation, two staples of any operations department. Ethan felt a bit like an animal in a zoo, surrounded by unfamiliar sights and sounds.

Megan, the team's workflow oracle, sat hunched over her dual monitors, her fingers flying across the keyboard with the speed and precision of a concert pianist. She didn't even blink as Ethan approached, her focus as unwavering as a laser beam. The screen was a riot of colors and numbers, a chaotic symphony of data that made Ethan's head spin. He recognized a few words – "KPI," "conversion rate," "ROI" – but they seemed to be swimming in a sea of acronyms and jargon. *It was like staring into the Matrix, but instead of green code, it was a spreadsheet from hell.*

"So, you're the new guy," she said, her voice smooth and detached, as if she were addressing a particularly unremarkable potted plant. "Fresh meat."

Ethan chuckled nervously, his grip on the notebook tightening. "That obvious?" he mumbled, trying to make himself as inconspicuous as possible, which was proving to be quite a challenge considering he was pretty sure his face was currently the same shade as a ripe tomato.

"Well," Megan said, not missing a keystroke, "considering you introduced yourself to Noah this morning with, and I quote, 'Slide into my DMs if you need me,' yeah, it's obvious."

Ethan groaned, dragging his hand down his face. His cheeks flushed an even deeper shade of red. "I'm never living that down, am I?" he muttered, wishing he could melt into the floor and become one with the industrial carpet.

Megan finally turned her chair to face him, her smirk dialed up to a level that practically radiated amusement. Her expression was one part teasing, two parts "rookie mistake," and a dash of "I've seen worse." "Nope. But hey, points for originality. One time, a guy kicked off his intro with a Game of Thrones quote. Noah didn't even blink."

Ethan raised an eyebrow, trying to suppress a grin. "What happened to him?"

"Oh, he didn't survive the Winter," Megan said, her voice dropping to a dramatic whisper. "Turns out, Operations isn't exactly the Iron Throne. You can't fake your way through it."

Ethan leaned against the desk, relaxing slightly. Megan's humor, sharp and unapologetic, felt oddly comforting amidst the chaos of his first day. "So... what, this is like bootcamp for corporate nerds?"

Megan tilted her head thoughtfully. "More like the engine room of the company. We keep things moving. Not flashy, but if we screw up, the whole ship sinks. And Noah's the captain, FYI. A terrifyingly efficient one."

Ethan nodded slowly, trying to process it all. Noah, the Operations manager, had already made an impression—primarily by critiquing Ethan's onboarding questions with the kind of bluntness that left no room for interpretation. Ethan had the feeling that Noah could make a performance review sound like a death sentence.

"So, basically... don't screw up?" he asked cautiously.

"Bingo," Megan said, swiveling back to her monitor. "Now, let's get you up to speed before Noah adds your name to his 'people to vaporize' list."

**The Workflow Gauntlet**

Megan spun her monitor toward Ethan, revealing a dashboard that looked like a rainbow had thrown up on a spreadsheet. Rows of data stretched endlessly, broken up by pie charts, bar graphs, and color-coded tags that practically screamed, "Corporate chaos—enter if you dare." Ethan felt a wave of nausea wash over him.

"This," Megan began, her voice taking on the tone of a seasoned tour guide leading a group through the Amazon rainforest, "is our QA tracking system. Think of it as the Bible of workflow management. You'll use it to monitor handoffs, flag issues, and make sure we don't miss deadlines. Precision is non-negotiable."

Ethan nodded, pretending to follow along, but his brain was already short-circuiting. Megan's words blurred into a stream of technical jargon: metrics, validation protocols, cross-team dependencies. He felt like a first-year med student staring at an open-heart surgery, except instead of a beating heart, it was a spreadsheet, and instead of blood, it was data, and instead of saving a life, he was... well, he wasn't sure what he was doing, but it seemed terrifyingly important.

By the time Megan explained "tagging protocols" for the third time, his confidence had flatlined. The panic in his chest was rising, threatening to drown out the rest of her explanation. His heart hammered against his ribs, his palms were slick with sweat, and he was pretty sure he was going to pass out. He stole a glance at his notebook, realizing his scribbled notes might as well have been hieroglyphics.

"You good?" Megan asked, raising an eyebrow. Her expression was a mix of concern and amusement, as if she could sense the storm brewing in his head.

"Totally," Ethan lied, giving her his most convincing thumbs-up. "Crystal clear."

Megan smirked, clearly unconvinced. She handed him a small dataset. "Here's your trial run. Follow the instructions. No shortcuts. I mean it."

Ethan nodded earnestly, but as soon as Megan walked off, he glanced at the instructions and thought, *How hard can it be? It's just a bunch of numbers and boxes. I can totally handle this.*

**The Shortcut That Backfired**

Fueled by a mix of overconfidence and desperation, Ethan decided to skip some of the "redundant" steps Megan had emphasized. He convinced himself that he was being efficient, not reckless. *They'll thank me later, he thought smugly. I'm a trailblazer, a pioneer of efficiency. They'll probably give me a promotion for this.*

An hour later, Megan returned, holding a printed report like it was evidence in a high-profile trial. Her expression was a mix of thunderclouds and impending doom.

"Ethan," she said, her tone teetering between disappointment and disbelief, "did you skip validation on this dataset?"

Ethan hesitated, the confidence draining from his face faster than air from a punctured tire. "Uh... yeah, but the data looked fine—"

"You figured wrong," Megan interrupted, her voice sharp enough to cut glass. "QA flagged an error. Now they have to redo part of the workflow, which sets us back."

"It's just one mistake," Ethan argued, his voice defensive. "I'll get it right next time."

Megan's expression hardened. "One mistake here ripples across teams, Ethan. You're not just messing up your work—you're messing up theirs too.

This isn't about saving time. It's about getting it right the first time."

She handed him a printed copy of the instructions, her eyes narrowing. "Follow this exactly. No shortcuts."

Ethan nodded, his earlier bravado crumbling like a poorly built Jenga tower. He felt the weight of Megan's words settling on his shoulders, heavier than he'd expected. He suddenly understood the phrase "soul-crushing."

**Noah Steps In**

As Ethan sat at his desk, replaying Megan's scolding in his head and wondering if he could fake a sudden illness to escape, a shadow loomed over him. He looked up to see Noah standing there, arms crossed like a judge ready to deliver a verdict. Ethan felt a chill run down his spine despite the fact that the office was a balmy 72 degrees.

"Problems?" Noah asked, his voice calm but carrying enough authority to make Ethan's palms sweat. He had the kind of presence that could silence a room full of screaming children with a single glance.

"Not anymore," Megan replied smoothly, stepping in like a lawyer defending her client. "Just a learning curve."

Noah's gaze shifted to Ethan, pinning him in place like a spotlight. *It was the kind of look that made you question every decision you'd made in the last 24 hours, including your choice of breakfast cereal.*

"Ethan," Noah said, his tone even but firm, "Operations isn't about creativity. It's about consistency. Shortcuts don't save time—they create risks. If you want to improve a process, you need to understand it first. Are we clear?"

Ethan swallowed hard and nodded. "Crystal."

Noah gave a single nod, his expression unreadable. "Good. Megan, let me know if he skips another step."

And just like that, Noah strode off, his presence leaving a chill in the air that had nothing to do with the AC.

Megan sighed, shaking her head. "Consider yourself lucky."

"Lucky?" Ethan repeated, incredulous.

"If Noah's giving you advice, it means he hasn't written you off yet," Megan explained. "He doesn't waste time on lost causes."

Ethan slumped in his chair, wondering how long it would take to prove he wasn't one. He also wondered if Noah had a secret "lost causes" list, and if it was color-coded.

**Late-Night Revelations**

That night, Ethan stayed late, his desk illuminated only by the glow of his monitor. The office had fallen silent, save for the faint hum of the AC and the occasional clatter of a coffee mug being washed in the breakroom. He felt like the last man on Earth, surrounded by the ghosts of spreadsheets past.

He stared at the printed instructions Megan had given him, his mind replaying the day's events. Every critique, every glance from Noah, every piece of advice from Megan—they all swirled together in his head, forming a cocktail of frustration and determination. He felt like he was drowning in a sea of data, but somewhere deep down, a tiny spark of defiance flickered.

He wanted to make an impact, to prove he wasn't just another rookie destined to crash and burn. But today, the grind had felt relentless, like trying to climb a mountain while the summit moved further away with every step. He thought about the vibrant energy of the Marketing department, the quiet focus of Product Development. *Were those teams facing the same struggles? Or was Operations uniquely designed to crush souls?*

Ethan took a deep breath, forcing himself to focus. There was a lesson buried in the chaos. If Noah's systems had kept the company afloat during its darkest days, maybe there was something to the rigidity. Maybe the rules weren't just there to hold him back—they were there to hold everything together. *Maybe Noah wasn't just a terrifyingly efficient robot; maybe he was a terrifyingly efficient robot with a purpose.*

**Lessons Learned (For Now)**

Ethan stared at the screen, his fingers hovering over the keyboard. He felt the weight of every decision, every keystroke. There was no room for shortcuts now—only precision and care. *No skipping. No guessing. Just get it right.* He thought about the error he'd made, the ripple effect it had caused. He wouldn't let that happen again.

For the first time, he understood the grind wasn't about perfection. It was about resilience. About showing up, doing the work, and earning your place—one painstaking step at a time. It was about understanding the system, mastering the rules, and then maybe, just maybe, finding a way to bend them.

Operations wasn't glamorous, but it was real. And for Ethan, that was enough. For now. He still wasn't sure if he belonged in this world of spreadsheets and deadlines, but he was determined to give it his best shot. He would learn the rules, master the tools, and maybe even impress Noah. *Or at least avoid getting vaporized by him.*

As he finally closed his laptop and headed out of the office, Ethan felt a strange mix of exhaustion and exhilaration. It had been a tough day, but he'd learned a lot. And he had a feeling that this was just the beginning of a very long, very challenging, and possibly very rewarding journey.

CHAPTER V

# First Big Fall

Ethan marched into the office the next morning, his jaw set, his eyes narrowed with focus. He wasn't going to let yesterday's mistake define him. He would prove to Noah, to Megan, and to himself that he could master this system. He would show them that he wasn't just some reckless kid with a knack for social media – he was a valuable asset to the team. He adjusted his messenger bag, the weight of it feeling reassuringly familiar. Today was a new day, a chance to start fresh.

He settled into his desk, the familiar hum of the office washing over him. Keyboards clacked, phones rang, and the low murmur of conversations filled the air. But today, the sounds didn't feel as chaotic. He was starting to recognize the rhythm of the place, the ebb and flow of the workday.

Rules are great and all, he thought, powering up his laptop. But creativity? That's where the magic happens. He wasn't going to abandon his instincts, his drive to innovate. But he would temper it with caution, with a newfound respect for the rules.

He opened the QA tracking system. It was as daunting as ever – rows of repetitive steps, validation prompts, and manual checks. But today, he saw it with new eyes. He saw the logic behind the steps, the importance of each check and balance. He saw the system not as a hindrance, but as a framework, a foundation upon which he could build.

Ethan stared at the screen, his mind racing. There had to be a better way. A faster way. A more efficient way. And then it hit him. An idea so simple, so obvious, it was a wonder no one had thought of it before. He would automate the error classification process. He would use the power of AI to streamline the workflow, to eliminate the tedious manual steps.

Heart pounding with excitement, Ethan opened ChatGPT. He typed furiously, his fingers flying across the keyboard:

"How can I automate error classification for a QA system? Need to optimize time and reduce manual steps. Must maintain accuracy and reliability."

The response came instantly, a wall of text filled with technical jargon and complex instructions. Ethan skimmed through it, his mind buzzing with possibilities. He saw the potential, the power of this technology. He would harness it, bend it to his will, and create something truly innovative.

Fueled by his newfound plan, Ethan worked tirelessly. He followed ChatGPT's instructions, deciphering the complex code, testing each step, and refining the process. He encountered roadblocks, moments of doubt, but he pushed through them, driven by a desire to prove himself, to show Noah and Megan that he was more than just a rookie.

He spent hours tweaking the code, testing the system, and refining the process. He lost track of time, the outside world fading away as he immersed himself in the challenge. He felt a thrill of excitement with each successful test, a surge of confidence with every hurdle overcome.

By lunchtime, Ethan felt like he was walking on air. He wasn't just keeping up with Operations – he was pushing it forward. He had created something new, something innovative, something that could potentially revolutionize the way they worked. He could barely contain his excitement.

Opening Slack, he fired off a message to the team that practically radiated self-satisfaction:

"Streamlined and automated! Faster and cleaner than before – check it out!"

He leaned back, imagining the praise that would pour in. *They're going to love this.* he thought. Noah might even crack a smile.

But the reality check came mid-afternoon, when Megan appeared at his desk holding a printout that looked suspiciously like an autopsy report. Her face was pale, her eyes wide with alarm.

"Ethan," she said, her voice trembling, "what exactly did you submit?"

Ethan straightened in his chair, flashing what he hoped was a confident smile. "It's an automated version of the workflow. It saves time and skips the repetitive parts."

Megan's expression darkened. "It skips the validation steps."

Ethan blinked. "Uh... yeah. But that's the point, right? Less repetition."

Megan sighed, her calm demeanor visibly cracking. "Half the dataset is flagged incorrectly. QA is scrambling to fix problems that didn't exist, and the actual errors are still sitting there, unaddressed."

Ethan's stomach lurched. The air thickened, the office walls seemed to close in on him. He could feel the blood draining from his face, his carefully constructed confidence crumbling like a stale cookie.

"Oh," he mumbled, his voice barely a whisper. "But I—"

"Don't," Megan interrupted, holding up a hand like a traffic cop. "I told you yesterday: no shortcuts. Validation is non-negotiable, Ethan. This isn't just a mistake – it's a disaster."

Ethan opened his mouth to defend himself, but Megan cut him off. "Let's see what Noah has to say about this."

**Facing the Music**

Megan didn't have to wait long. Noah materialized at Ethan's desk not ten minutes later, his expression unreadable but his presence heavy enough to make the air feel ten degrees colder. Ethan felt a wave of nausea wash over him. He was pretty sure he was going to throw up.

"Ethan," Noah began, his voice like ice shards, "explain what happened."

Ethan stumbled over his words, trying to condense his process without sounding completely reckless. "I thought... I thought automation would help. I tested it on a small dataset, and it worked. I didn't realize—"

"That it would fall apart when scaled up?" Noah finished, his voice still calm but laced with a chilling disappointment. "Automation isn't magic. If you don't test every part of the process, you're not streamlining – you're guessing."

Ethan winced. "I just wanted to make it better."

Noah stared at him for a long moment, his gaze piercing, then glanced at Megan. "How bad is the damage?"

"QA is still untangling it," Megan replied. "But we've lost hours."

Noah's gaze was like a laser beam, burning into Ethan's skin. The air crackled with tension. Ethan felt another wave of nausea wash over him.

"Ethan, this isn't a sandbox. Operations isn't a place for untested ideas or half-baked solutions. Every mistake here ripples outward – to QA, to fulfillment, to the client."

Ethan nodded, his throat dry. "I get it."

"Do you?" Noah asked, his tone hardening. "Because this is the second time this week you've skipped steps. If I can't trust you to follow instructions, why should I trust you with bigger responsibilities?"

Ethan felt like the floor had been pulled out from under him. His gaze dropped to the floor, his cheeks burning with shame. He felt like a child being scolded by a disappointed parent. He wanted to disappear, to melt into the industrial carpet and become one with the office furniture. He nodded mutely, too ashamed to meet Noah's eyes.

Noah straightened. "Fix this. Shadow Megan until you understand every part of the process. And next time you want to 'innovate,' ask first."

With that, Noah turned and walked away, leaving Ethan feeling like a deflated balloon.

Megan's Perspective

After Noah left, Megan sighed, leaning against the edge of her desk. "You've got guts, I'll give you that," she said. "But guts don't matter if you're not willing to do the work."

Ethan managed a weak smile. "You think Noah's always been this intense?"

Megan chuckled. "Oh, he has. But he's intense because he cares. Back when SynergyWorks was on the brink of collapse, it was Noah who kept the ship afloat. He practically lived in the office, poring over spreadsheets, identifying inefficiencies, and streamlining workflows. He saw firsthand the cost of mistakes, the impact they had on the company, on the clients, on people's livelihoods. He's not just a stickler for rules – he's a guardian of stability."

Ethan raised an eyebrow. "So he's... a perfectionist?"

Megan shook her head. "He's not chasing perfection. He's chasing reliability. And if you want to be part of this team, you need to understand the difference."

**Mila and Noah's Conversation**

Later that evening, as the office lights dimmed and the usual bustle subsided, Mila found Noah standing by the window, gazing out at the cityscape. The city lights twinkled below, a stark contrast to the quiet intensity in his eyes.

Mila was a senior manager at SynergyWorks, a veteran of the tech world who had seen it all. She was known for her sharp wit, her ability to navigate complex situations, and her knack for understanding people. She was also one of the few people who could challenge Noah without fear, a testament to their long history and mutual respect.

"Got a minute?" Mila asked, her voice gentle but firm.

Noah turned, his expression unreadable. "Depends. What's on your mind?"

"Ethan," Mila said simply.

Noah's frown deepened. "What about him?"

Mila crossed her arms. "You're coming down on him too hard. He's got potential, but you're making him feel like every mistake is the end of the world."

"He needs to learn," Noah replied, his tone clipped. "Accountability isn't optional in Operations. One mistake here ripples outward. You know that as well as I do."

"Of course, I do," Mila said. "But you're missing the point. He's still figuring things out. Let him fail, sure – but don't make him so afraid to try that he stops altogether. He's creative, Noah. That's rare in Operations. Give him some space to learn without feeling like he's one mistake away from being benched."

Noah leaned back against the windowsill, folding his arms. "Creativity is valuable, but not when it comes at the expense of reliability. We don't have the luxury of tolerating reckless mistakes."

"Reckless?" Mila arched an eyebrow. "He's not reckless. He's over-eager. There's a difference. He's trying to impress you, not sabotage the workflow."

Noah exhaled sharply. "Mila, do you know what it's like to manage a team that's been burned by carelessness? To explain to a client why their deliverable is late because someone decided to 'streamline' without thinking it through?"

"Of course, I do," Mila said evenly. "But I also know what it's like to see someone with promise give up because their manager couldn't see past a mistake. That's not you, Noah. At least, it shouldn't be."

Noah looked at her, his jaw tightening. "You think I'm being too harsh?"

"I think," Mila said, choosing her words carefully, "that you're holding him to a standard he doesn't even understand yet. He's new. He needs time to learn the rules before he can follow them perfectly. Give him a chance to grow into the role, or you'll lose him before he has the chance to prove himself."

Noah stared out the window, the city lights reflecting in his eyes. "I don't want him to stop taking risks," he admitted finally. "But risks without preparation? That's dangerous – for him and the team."

"Agreed," Mila said. "But preparation takes time. He's starting to get it, Noah. Trust me. Give him a little room to fail without the weight of the world on his shoulders."

Noah was quiet for a long moment, his expression unreadable. Finally, he nodded, though it wasn't exactly a gesture of agreement.

"I'll think about it," he said.

Mila smiled faintly. "That's all I'm asking."

Noah watched as she walked away, then looked back out the window, the city lights blurring into a sea of possibilities. He wasn't the type to second-guess himself, but Mila's words lingered, threading into his thoughts like a quiet echo.

*Maybe she's right, he thought reluctantly. But I can't let him think this job is just trial and error. He needs to understand the stakes.*

As he headed back to his desk, the familiar weight of responsibility settled on his shoulders. For all his insistence on precision and accountability, Noah couldn't shake the flicker of recognition he felt when he looked at Ethan. Once upon a time, he'd been just as eager, just as determined – and just as prone to mistakes. He remembered the sting of criticism, the frustration of setbacks. He remembered the mentors who had guided him, the ones who had believed in him even when he doubted himself. Maybe, just maybe, he could be that for Ethan.

**Reflection**

Ethan spent the rest of the day untangling the mess he'd made. This time, he tested every step, triple-checked the validation process, and followed Megan's original workflow like it was gospel. By evening, he submitted a corrected version, his heart pounding with a mix of anxiety and hope.

Megan nodded when he handed it over. "Better," she said. It wasn't high praise, but it felt like a lifeline.

As he packed up, Mila's words stuck with him: "Noah values accountability because it builds trust."

*Lesson learned, he thought. Accountability might not be as fun as innovation, but apparently, it's a thing adults care about. Who knew?*

He left the office that night feeling exhausted but strangely exhilarated. He had made a mistake, a big one, but he had learned from it. He had faced the consequences, and he had come out stronger on the other side. He was starting to understand the delicate balance between innovation and accountability, between taking risks and following the rules. And he was starting to realize that maybe, just maybe, he could find his place in this world after all.

CHAPTER VI

# Balancing Work and Life

Ethan fidgeted with his pen, the smooth metal a stark contrast to the rough texture of the workflow document on his screen. The words blurred into a sea of meaningless jargon, his gaze drifting towards the window. The cityscape stretched out before him, a concrete jungle teeming with life, a stark contrast to the sterile environment of the office. His mind was elsewhere, drawn to the steady ping of his group chat, each notification a tempting invitation to a world outside of spreadsheets and deadlines.

Brad: "Cabin escape this weekend. Let's do it. Nature + no deadlines = perfect reset."

Jess: "Please. I need this. My brain is fried."

Brad: "Ethan, you in?"

Ethan closed his eyes, picturing the scene: a cozy cabin nestled in the woods, a crackling fire, the smell of pine needles and roasted marshmallows. He could almost hear the laughter of his friends, the crackling of the fire, the gentle rustling of leaves. It was a siren song, a tempting escape from the relentless grind of the office.

But then his gaze fell on the folder Megan had handed him earlier that morning, marked with bold red letters: "Review Required by Monday."

His stomach lurched. The blood drained from his face, his carefully constructed composure crumbling like a poorly built sandcastle. He could feel the weight of Noah's disapproval bearing down on him, crushing his newfound confidence.

He hadn't forgotten Noah's warning from earlier in the week: "Accountability doesn't take weekends off." And after his blunder with the workflow automation, the last thing he wanted was another black mark on his record.

"Hey," Zara's voice startled him. She walked past, balancing a stack of files that seemed to defy gravity. "You okay? You look... conflicted."

Ethan forced a smile, his cheeks aching from the effort. "Just debating the meaning of life."

Zara snorted. "Good luck with that. Let me know if you figure it out."

**The Internal Debate**

For the next hour, Ethan sat frozen in place, his mind a battleground of conflicting thoughts and emotions.

*If I don't go, I'm letting everyone down.* he thought. *They'll think I'm boring, a workaholic, a corporate drone. I'll become 'that guy' who always chooses spreadsheets over friends.*

But then the other side of the argument would rear its head.

*But if I do go and miss this deadline, Noah will have my head,* he imagined Noah's disappointed frown, his sharp words cutting through Ethan's carefully constructed confidence. He'll think I'm irresponsible, unreliable, not ready for the challenges of Operations. He might even fire me.

Another ping pulled him out of his spiral:

Jess: "Ethan? Don't ghost us. Are you coming or not?"

Ethan hovered over the keyboard, his fingers trembling.

*I need this break,* he thought. *I need to recharge, to reconnect with the world outside of work. I need to laugh, to relax, to remember what it feels like to be a human being, not just a cog in the corporate machine.*

But then the folder on his desk would catch his eye, its bold red letters a stark reminder of his responsibilities.

*I can't let the team down, he thought. I can't afford another mistake. I need to prove myself, to show Noah that I'm capable, that I'm reliable, that I'm worthy of his trust.*

The internal debate raged on, each side vying for control, each thought a tug-of-war between his personal needs and his professional obligations.

**The Decision**

By lunchtime, Ethan's focus was hanging by a thread. The unopened folder on his desk sat there like an ominous to-do list, its bold red letters glaring at him every time he glanced in its direction. His group chat, meanwhile, buzzed with relentless excitement, pulling his attention back like a magnet.

Brad: "Dude. Work will still be there Monday. You, however, need this. Don't make me guilt-trip you."

Ethan groaned aloud, sinking lower into his chair. His rational side screamed: *Stay and finish the review! It's two days of work versus one weekend of fun.*

But his emotional side, the one tired of spreadsheets and Noah's relentless expectations, whispered: *Do it. Take the trip. You'll figure out Monday when you get there.*

Ethan leaned back in his chair, staring at the ceiling. The fluorescent lights flickered overhead, casting a sterile glow on the office. He felt trapped, suffocated by the weight of his responsibilities.

*What's the worst that could happen?* he thought. Besides disappointing Noah. And Megan. And maybe derailing the meeting. *Okay, those are all bad, but seriously, when's the last time I had a real weekend?* When's the last time I did something for myself, something that wasn't about work, about proving myself, about meeting someone else's expectations?

Finally, he slammed his hands on the desk, startling Zara as she passed by.

"Everything okay over there?" she asked, raising an eyebrow.

"Yeah," Ethan said, sitting up straighter. "Just making an important life decision."

"Uh-huh," Zara replied, clearly unconvinced. But she didn't press further, sensing the internal battle raging within him.

With a burst of impulsive energy, Ethan grabbed his phone and opened the chat.

"Fine. I'm in. Pick me up at 6."

Brad's reply was instant: "Knew you'd come around. Pack snacks!"

Ethan closed the chat and glanced once more at the unopened folder on his desk. It sat there, accusing him silently.

"I'll deal with it later," he muttered, shoving the folder aside as if that would solve the problem.

As the clock ticked closer to the end of the day, Ethan tried not to think about Monday – or Noah – or the fact that this decision felt like playing emotional roulette. Instead, he clung to the idea that bonfires, nature, and a weekend with friends would recharge him enough to tackle anything.

*Future me can handle it, he thought. Right?*

**The Weekend Escape**

The cabin was everything Ethan had hoped for: crisp mountain air, stars visible without light pollution, and the kind of relaxed energy only a weekend escape with friends could offer. They spent their days hiking through the woods, their evenings huddled around the fire, sharing stories, laughter, and the occasional questionable campfire song. Ethan felt the tension drain from his shoulders, the weight of responsibility lifting with each breath of fresh air.

But the peace didn't last long.

It started on the second night, as they sat around the fire, the flames casting dancing shadows on their faces. Brad tossed a marshmallow onto a stick and grinned at Ethan. "So, new guy. What's it like working for SynergyWorks? Heard you've got a boss who's basically a human buzzkill."

Ethan snorted. "You mean Noah? He's... intense."

Jess leaned forward, her eyes gleaming with mischief. "Define 'intense.' Like, scary intense? Or 'sends emails at 2 AM' intense?"

"Both," Ethan replied, laughing. "He's the kind of guy who probably alphabetizes his email folders and cross-references them with a spreadsheet."

Brad nearly choked on his marshmallow. "And you're surviving this how?"

Ethan shrugged. "Barely. Honestly, it feels like I'm constantly one mistake away from getting benched."

Jess tilted her head. "But isn't that kind of the point? You're new. You're supposed to mess up."

Ethan groaned. "Tell that to Noah. His motto might as well be 'Perfection or nothing.'"

"That's ridiculous," Brad said, shaking his head. "Look, work is important, but if it's stressing you out this much, maybe it's not worth it. What's the worst that happens if you mess up? You get fired? There are other jobs."

Jess nodded. "Exactly. Work to live, not live to work. Right?"

Ethan hesitated. "I mean, yeah, but... it's not that simple. Operations isn't just spreadsheets – it's about making sure the whole company runs smoothly. If I mess up, it's not just my mistake. It affects the team, the clients... it's a lot of pressure."

"Pressure you didn't ask for," Brad pointed out.

"Or maybe it's pressure he needs," Jess countered, raising an eyebrow at Brad. "Some people thrive under it."

"Yeah, some people," Ethan said, throwing a marshmallow into the fire and watching it blacken and shrivel. "Not me. Not yet, anyway."

Brad leaned back, grinning. "Well, if you ever want to quit and join the 'screw work' lifestyle, let me know. I've got a hammock with your name on it."

Ethan laughed, but the conversation left him uneasy. *Am I doing this wrong? Should I be leaning into the grind or stepping back? Am I prioritizing the wrong things? Am I letting my fear of failure hold me back from truly experiencing life?*

He didn't have an answer by the time the weekend ended. But for now, the stars, the laughter, and the crackling fire offered a brief escape from the weight of responsibility.

**Monday Morning Reality Check**

The alarm clock ripped Ethan from a dream about spreadsheets chasing him through a forest of kombucha bottles. He groaned, the remnants of the weekend's peace clinging to him like a fading scent. He'd woken up feeling refreshed, the cabin trip a distant memory already fading under the harsh reality of Monday morning.

He stumbled into the office, the familiar smell of stale coffee and desperation hitting him like a wave. The weekend's carefree energy evaporated, replaced by a knot of anxiety in his stomach.

That knot tightened when Megan approached, her expression a mix of exhaustion and frustration.

"Morning, Ethan," she said tersely. "Quick question: did you finish the workflow review?"

Ethan's stomach lurched. The blood drained from his face, his carefully constructed composure crumbling like a poorly built sandcastle. He could feel the weight of Noah's disapproval bearing down on him, crushing his newfound confidence.

"I, uh... was going to do it this morning," he stammered, his voice cracking.

Megan closed her eyes for a beat, exhaling sharply. "Great. Well, Noah needed it for his 9 AM meeting, so you'd better hope he's in a forgiving mood."

Ethan's pulse quickened. He grabbed the folder from his desk and scrambled to make sense of the contents, his fingers fumbling over the keyboard as he tried to catch up. The words swam before his eyes, the numbers blurring into a meaningless jumble. Panic clawed at his throat, threatening to choke him.

**The Confrontation**

Noah didn't wait for Ethan to come to him. He appeared at Ethan's desk just as the clock struck 10, his expression unreadable but his presence enough to make Ethan's pulse race.

"Ethan," Noah said evenly, his tone calm but firm, "can we talk?"

Ethan felt the weight of the entire room's gaze as he stood and followed Noah into a nearby conference room. The door shut behind them with a soft click that sounded louder than it should have.

Noah gestured toward a chair, but Ethan hesitated before sitting, feeling like a student summoned to the principal's office.

"Care to explain why the workflow review wasn't ready this morning?" Noah asked, his voice sharp enough to cut through Ethan's carefully rehearsed defenses.

Ethan shifted uncomfortably, his mind scrambling for the right words. "I was going to finish it first thing today, but..."

"But?" Noah prompted, raising an eyebrow.

Ethan exhaled, the truth tumbling out before he could second-guess it. "I went on a trip this weekend. I needed a break. I figured I'd have time to catch up today."

Noah stared at him for a long moment, the silence heavy and unyielding. "You figured wrong," he said finally. "This isn't just about you, Ethan. Your delay affected the entire team's ability to prepare for this morning's meeting. Accountability doesn't stop because you need a break."

Ethan bristled at the implication. "So what, Noah? We're just supposed to work non-stop and burn ourselves out? Is that really better for the team in the long run?"

Noah's eyes narrowed, his voice taking on a harder edge. "Burnout is real, but so is responsibility. The difference is knowing when to prioritize the team over yourself. If you can't do that, how can I trust you?"

Ethan clenched his fists under the table, willing himself to stay calm. "Maybe if this place didn't treat every task like a life-or-death situation, people wouldn't burn out in the first place."

Noah leaned forward, his gaze unflinching. "Work-life balance doesn't mean abandoning your commitments, Ethan. It means managing them responsibly. Balance isn't about taking breaks whenever you feel like it – it's about understanding when you can and when you can't. If you want to be part of this team, that's non-negotiable."

The words hit Ethan like a punch to the gut. He wanted to argue, to push back, but deep down, he knew Noah wasn't entirely wrong. He had let the team down, and that realization stung.

Noah straightened, the momentary tension in his posture fading. "Here's what's going to happen," he said, his tone brisk. "You're going to finish that review by the end of the day. And next time you feel the need to 'recharge,' you're going to make sure your work is covered first. Understood?"

Ethan nodded mutely, his jaw tight.

"Good," Noah said. "You can go."

As Ethan left the conference room, he felt a strange mix of anger and guilt. He knew he'd made a mistake, but Noah's words still felt like an attack, like he was expected to give everything to the job without question.

**Ethan's Reflection**

Back at his desk, Ethan slumped back in his chair, the weight of the confrontation pressing down on him. He felt a strange mix of anger and guilt, frustration and confusion. He had made a mistake, but was it really so unforgivable? Was he really expected to sacrifice his entire life for this job?

He opened the workflow review and got to work, his fingers moving automatically while his mind replayed the confrontation.

*Accountability doesn't stop because you need a break.*

The words echoed in his head, gnawing at him. He hated feeling like he'd let the team down, but he also couldn't shake the frustration bubbling under the surface.

*Was Noah right? Did accountability really mean sacrificing your personal time whenever work demanded it? Or was this just corporate culture disguised as responsibility?*

The thought nagged at him as he typed. When he finally couldn't take it anymore, he grabbed his notebook and opened to a blank page.

At the top, he wrote: Where's the line?

Underneath, he started jotting questions:

Is work-life balance even real?

How do you balance personal needs with professional ones?

Can you be a "team player" without losing yourself in the process?

Does Noah ever take a break? Seriously, does he?

He paused, staring at the last question, and let out a frustrated sigh.

*"Oh hey, you, silently judging me from your side of the page: What would you do?"* he muttered under his breath. "Pick the grind or take the break? Because right now, I'm stuck in the middle."

He tapped the pen against the notebook absently. He knew Noah wasn't entirely wrong – he should've planned better. But it still felt like there was something fundamentally unfair about the way work seemed to demand everything without compromise.

Ethan sighed again, flipping the notebook shut and shoving it back into his bag.

*I don't have all the answers yet,* he thought. *But maybe that's okay for now. Maybe figuring it out is part of the process.*

For the rest of the day, Ethan chipped away at the review, his resolve quietly steeling itself. If nothing else, he was determined not to let himself or the team down again. He would find a way to balance his personal needs with his professional responsibilities, even if it meant navigating a minefield of conflicting expectations. He would find a way to be both accountable and human, even if it meant challenging the norms of the corporate world.

## CHAPTER VII

# Building Trust

Ethan's shoulders stiffened, his grip on his pen tightening. He could feel Noah's gaze on him, a silent weight that made him acutely aware of every move, every breath. The air crackled with a tension he hadn't noticed before, a subtle undercurrent of expectation that seemed to emanate from Noah's very presence.

"Morning, Ethan," Noah said, his voice devoid of the warmth Michael seemed to radiate like an over-caffeinated space heater. It was a voice that commanded attention, a voice that brooked no nonsense.

"Good morning!" Ethan responded, a touch too eagerly, his voice betraying the nervousness he was trying so hard to conceal. He shifted in his chair, suddenly aware of how his casual posture clashed with Noah's crisp, efficient demeanor.

Noah placed a slim folder on Ethan's desk with the precision of someone delivering a subpoena. Each movement was deliberate, measured, as if even the slightest deviation from the plan could have disastrous consequences. "I've got a task for you," he said, his tone brooking no argument.

Ethan eyed the folder suspiciously, like it might bite. He'd learned that in Operations, even inanimate objects seemed to carry the potential for disaster. "Sure. What's the task?" he asked, trying to sound nonchalant, but his voice wavered slightly.

"We're finalizing a quarterly client report," Noah explained, his tone businesslike. "Your job is to cross-check the operational metrics in this draft with the database. Every number must be accurate. Mark discrepancies, flag anything that seems off, and make sure your notes are clear."

Ethan flipped open the folder, revealing a spreadsheet that seemed to stretch on forever, a dense jungle of numbers and formulas. The spreadsheet stretched out before him like an endless desert of numbers, each cell a potential trap, each row a minefield of potential errors. Ethan's eyes burned, his head throbbed, and he could feel his sanity slowly slipping away. He swallowed hard, his initial confidence faltering. But he couldn't let Noah see his doubt, his fear. He had to project an image of competence, of control.

"Got it," he said, forcing a confident smile. "Sounds like a challenge."

Noah's gaze lingered just long enough to make Ethan squirm. "This isn't just about numbers. It's about precision. We can't afford mistakes in a client report."

*Translation: Don't screw this up.*

"Understood," Ethan replied with a firm nod, though his stomach churned as Noah walked away. He could feel the weight of responsibility settling on his shoulders, heavy and suffocating.

**The Grind**

Ethan spread the contents of the folder across his desk, the pages fanning out like the wings of an intimidating data hawk. He pulled up the database on his monitor and dove in, determined to prove himself. He meticulously compared each figure, each percentage, each decimal point, his red pen hovering over the page like a hawk.

At first, it seemed straightforward – match the numbers, flag errors, and move on. But as the hours wore on, the task became a relentless grind. The numbers swam before his eyes, blurring into a meaningless jumble. His head throbbed, his vision swam, and he could feel his focus slipping.

*Why am I doing this manually? he thought, frustration gnawing at him. Isn't there software that could handle this in, like, three clicks? Why are we stuck in the Stone Age of data analysis?*

He let out a frustrated sigh, stretching his arms above his head. His desk neighbor glanced over, raising an eyebrow. Ethan quickly dropped his arms and refocused, his cheeks burning with shame.

Then it happened. A mismatch.

Ethan's eyes widened. There it was, a glaring inconsistency, a rogue number hiding in plain sight. The spreadsheet seemed to mock him, its rows and columns a testament to his fallibility. His heart pounded in his chest, a mix of triumph and terror.

Gotcha, he muttered, marking the error with a red pen like he'd just won a game of Data Detective. But the victory was short-lived.

As he stared at the discrepancy, doubt began to creep in.

*What if there are more mistakes I missed? Should I go back and recheck the entire thing? What if this one error is just the tip of a giant, data-mess iceberg?*

He leaned back in his chair, chewing on the cap of his pen. The hours seemed to simultaneously crawl and speed by, his brain spiraling into overanalysis.

Finally, he sighed and muttered under his breath,

*"Hey, ever feel like one mistake makes you question your entire life? No? Just me? Cool."*

Determined not to let the task get the better of him, Ethan went back to the top of the report and started over. This time, he moved slower, his red pen working overtime as he cross-checked every figure. He scrutinized each number, each decimal point, each formula, his mind a whirlwind of calculations and comparisons.

**A Moment of Doubt**

By the time he reached the bottom of the report for the second time, Ethan's confidence was hanging by a thread. He had flagged three more discrepancies, each one sending a fresh wave of doubt washing over him.

*Am I actually catching these mistakes, or am I creating problems that don't exist? Am I overthinking this? Am I going to get fired for being too meticulous?*

He leaned back in his chair, rubbing his temples. His mind wandered to the folder's ominous "precision" warning and Noah's lingering words: We can't afford mistakes.

The stakes felt enormous, like one missed number could unravel the entire company. He could practically see the headlines: "SynergyWorks Collapses Due to Intern's Typo."

*Okay, that's dramatic. he thought. But still, what if I miss something important? What if I'm the reason the company goes bankrupt? What if I end up living in a cardboard box, subsisting on ramen noodles and regret?*

His finger hovered over the print button as he debated whether to double-check it all again. He groaned quietly, letting his head fall onto the desk for a moment. The cool surface against his forehead offered a brief respite from the mental turmoil.

When he sat back up, he whispered to himself, *"It's just a report. Not a manifesto. Nobody's going to frame it and hang it in a museum."*

Ethan forced himself to take a deep breath and hit print. The soft whir of the office printer filled the room as he gathered the marked-up pages. He stared at them, a mix of pride and trepidation swirling within him.

**Coffee and Clarity**

Two hours, three flagged discrepancies, and one existential crisis later, Ethan's brain felt like a fried circuit. The spreadsheet stared back at him like a digital void, and his red pen looked like it had been through the wars. He pushed back from his desk, resisting the urge to dramatically flop onto the floor.

Time for caffeine, he thought. And maybe a life reboot while I'm at it.

The break area was buzzing with its usual mid-morning crowd – people clutching coffee mugs like lifelines and making small talk about weekend plans and corporate gossip. Ethan beelined for the coffee machine, where Mila was refilling her ever-present tumbler.

Mila was a force of nature, a whirlwind of energy and ideas. She was known for her sharp wit, her ability to cut through the corporate BS, and her unwavering support for her team. She was also one of the few people who could make Noah laugh, a feat that Ethan considered nothing short of miraculous.

She glanced at him, her expression a mix of amusement and empathy. "Whoa. You look like you just fought a spreadsheet and lost."

"Data cross-checking," Ethan groaned, grabbing a mug and pouring himself whatever the coffee machine decided to produce. "It's like staring into the abyss, but instead of finding meaning, you find... typos."

Mila chuckled, her tumbler raised in a mock toast. "Welcome to Operations. Where typos are mortal sins and Noah is the high priest of accuracy. Remember what I said about not seeing numbers in your dreams?"

Ethan took a sip of his coffee and immediately regretted it. "This tastes like regret and missed opportunities. Perfect metaphor for my morning. And yeah, I remember. Guess I should've listened."

Mila leaned against the counter, smirking. "Noah give you the task?"

"Yeah," Ethan said, glancing at his mug like it might offer better advice than the internet. "Feels like a test. Like he's waiting for me to mess up so he can swoop in with a 'teachable moment.'"

"Because it is a test," Mila replied, her tone matter-of-fact. "That's Noah's thing. He wants to see if you can handle the basics without breaking a sweat. The guy doesn't trust people easily – he's probably had the same barber since 2010."

Ethan snorted. "So, what? I pass if I don't burn the place down?"

"Pretty much," Mila said. "But don't overthink it. Just get it right. And whatever you do, don't mess it up – Noah hates rework."

Ethan groaned dramatically. "Cool. No pressure. I'll just take my perfectly calm self back to my desk and cross-check data like my entire self-worth depends on it."

Mila grinned. "You're catching on."

He leaned in slightly. "But seriously, why am I doing this manually? Shouldn't there be software that handles this?"

Mila shrugged. "Probably. But software doesn't validate itself, and someone still has to make sure the numbers make sense. That's you – our human insurance policy."

"Great," Ethan muttered. "Love being the safety net."

"It's not so bad," Mila said. "Think of it this way: you're the guy who keeps everything from collapsing. That's a big deal."

Ethan arched an eyebrow. "Do I at least get a cape? Or maybe a raise?"

Mila laughed, pushing off the counter. "You get the satisfaction of knowing you didn't let Noah down. Isn't that enough?"

"Not remotely," Ethan shot back, grinning despite himself.

Mila shook her head, her tumbler in hand. "You'll survive. Just don't start seeing numbers in your dreams – it's a slippery slope."

**Delivery Time**

With the completed report in hand, Ethan made his way to Noah's desk, each step feeling heavier than the last. Noah was typing something on his laptop, his expression as unreadable as ever. Ethan's breath hitched. The air thickened, the office walls seemed to close in on him. He could feel the weight of Noah's expectations bearing down on him, crushing his newfound confidence.

"Here's the report," Ethan said, placing it on Noah's desk, his voice wavering slightly.

Noah glanced at the folder, then at Ethan. "You're confident it's accurate?"

Ethan hesitated for a fraction of a second. *This is the part where I either shine or crash and burn.*

"Yes," he said firmly, summoning every ounce of courage he could muster. "I double-checked everything."

Noah nodded, picking up the folder. "Good. I'll review it before the final submission."

Ethan exhaled quietly and turned to leave, feeling like he'd just completed a boss battle in a video game. As he walked back to his desk, a wave of relief washed over him – but it was tempered by the nagging thought that this was just one small task in a much larger game.

*Small but significant, he thought. One step at a time.*

**Reflection**

Ethan leaned back in his chair, exhaustion washing over him like a tidal wave. But beneath the fatigue, there was a sense of accomplishment, a quiet satisfaction that he had faced the challenge and emerged victorious. He had proven himself, not just to Noah, but to himself.

*"Okay, so maybe I'm not taking over Operations just yet. But hey – baby steps, right? Today, I conquered spreadsheets. Tomorrow... who knows? Maybe the whole client report."*

He paused, glancing toward Noah's desk. *"Although, I should probably hold off on pitching my 'world domination' plans to him. Let's not push my luck."*

Ethan opened a blank document on his laptop. As he began jotting down ideas for streamlining future workflows, he realized something surprising: the day hadn't been a total grind. Sure, the task had been tedious, but finishing it – and doing it well – felt oddly satisfying.

*"Trust isn't given – it's earned,"* Ethan muttered, almost echoing Noah's unspoken mantra. *"Guess I'll keep earning it. One spreadsheet at a time."*

He smiled, a genuine smile this time, not the forced grin he'd worn earlier in the day. He was starting to understand the rhythm of Operations, the importance of precision, the value of accountability. He was starting to see that even the most tedious tasks could hold a sense of purpose, a sense of accomplishment. And he was starting to believe that maybe, just maybe, he could find his place in this world after all.

## CHAPTER VIII

# Noah is human?

Ethan's heart skipped a beat. He turned slowly, his fingers tightening around the edge of his desk, his carefully constructed composure threatening to crack under the weight of Noah's scrutiny. The air crackled with a tension he hadn't noticed before, a subtle undercurrent of expectation that seemed to emanate from Noah's very presence. It was like the air pressure in the room had suddenly dropped, leaving Ethan feeling slightly breathless.

"Do you have an update on the client metrics report?" Noah's voice was calm, even, but it held a subtle edge that sent a shiver down Ethan's spine.

Ethan's mind raced. The client metrics report. The deadline. Friday, right? He'd been so focused on the other tasks, the endless stream of data and deadlines, that he'd completely forgotten about it.

"I thought the deadline was Friday," he mumbled, his voice barely a whisper.

Noah's jaw tightened, the slightest hint of disapproval flickering across his face. "I mentioned it during Monday's sync. It's due tomorrow. We discussed this."

Ethan's stomach lurched. The blood drained from his face, his carefully constructed confidence crumbling like a stale cookie. He could feel the weight of Noah's disapproval bearing down on him, crushing his newfound confidence.

Had he missed it? Was he zoning out again during one of Noah's bullet-point-heavy updates? Was he really that incompetent?

"I—I must've misunderstood," he stammered, cursing himself for sounding defensive. He wanted to explain, to justify, but the words caught in his throat.

Noah's gaze was like a laser beam, burning into Ethan's skin. The air crackled with tension. Ethan felt a wave of nausea wash over him. He was pretty sure he was going to throw up.

"Misunderstanding doesn't change the deadline. This isn't just about you – it impacts the entire team. Fix it." Noah's voice was still calm, but there was an underlying steeliness that made Ethan flinch.

Ethan swallowed hard, the knot of anxiety in his stomach tightening. "I can stay late tonight and get it done," he offered, trying to sound proactive, though his voice betrayed a hint of desperation.

"Do what you need to do," Noah said, his tone clipped as he turned and walked away. Ethan could feel the weight of his gaze even after he was gone, a lingering reminder of his failure.

Ethan slumped back in his chair, the weight of the missed deadline pressing down on him like a physical burden. He could feel the frustration bubbling up inside him, threatening to spill over. He wanted to scream, to throw something, to disappear. But instead, he took a deep breath and forced himself to focus.

*I can fix this*, he thought, his jaw clenching with determination. I can still meet the deadline. I just need to focus, to work smart, to push through the panic.

**The Sprint Against Time**

Ethan stared at his laptop, his mind racing faster than his fingers could type. He hadn't even opened the report yet, and already the pressure was building. His inner voice was split into two warring factions:

*How did I miss this? Am I really cut out for this job? Maybe I'm not as organized as I thought I was.*

*I can still fix it. I can prove myself. I can show Noah that I'm capable of handling this.*

He cracked his knuckles, a nervous habit he'd picked up in college, and opened the file. The spreadsheet was predictably dense, packed with metrics, client-specific jargon, and enough tabs to make his browser jealous. But this time, the complexity didn't intimidate him. He'd spent the past few weeks immersed in data, learning the language of Operations, and he was starting to feel a sense of familiarity, even mastery.

Time ticked by as Ethan cross-checked numbers, his red pen flying over notes. He flagged discrepancies, recalculated metrics, and triple-checked every entry. He was in the zone, his focus laser-sharp, his mind a whirlwind of calculations and comparisons.

By the third hour, his energy was starting to waver. He glanced at the clock – 4 PM. Still time to finish.

*But can I? The doubt crept in again, insidious and persistent. What if I'm not fast enough? What if I make a mistake? What if I let the team down again?*

He shoved aside the doubt, fueled by a mix of adrenaline and determination. *I can do this*, he thought, his fingers flying across the keyboard. *I will do this.*

Every time he caught an error, he felt a small surge of triumph, like a video game player hitting a checkpoint. But for every victory, his mind whispered, What if you missed something bigger? What if there's a critical flaw hidden somewhere in this data, waiting to sabotage your efforts?

At 6 PM, most of the office began clearing out, their goodbyes echoing faintly across the open floor plan. Ethan barely noticed. His desk was a battlefield – sticky notes, printouts, and a coffee mug he didn't remember emptying. The outside world faded away, the only reality the glowing screen in front of him, the only sounds the click of his keyboard and the whir of his brain.

By 8:30 PM, he leaned back, stretching his aching shoulders and staring at the finished report. The numbers were perfect, or at least as perfect as he could make them. He printed the final copy and placed it neatly in the folder.

"Done," he muttered, a mix of exhaustion and pride washing over him. He'd done it. He'd met the deadline, despite the setback, despite the doubt. He'd proven himself, not just to Noah, but to himself.

**The Next Morning**

Ethan arrived early, the report clutched in his hand like a trophy. He walked to Noah's desk, his heart pounding as he placed it down. He could feel Noah's gaze on him, assessing, evaluating.

"Here's the report," he said, his voice steady despite the nerves bubbling underneath.

Noah glanced at the folder, then at Ethan. "You confident it's accurate?"

Ethan nodded firmly. "Yes. I double-checked everything."

Noah opened the folder and flipped through a few pages, his expression unreadable. Ethan held his breath, waiting for the verdict.

Finally, Noah nodded. "Good work."

It wasn't effusive praise, but for Noah, it was practically a standing ovation. Ethan felt a surge of relief, a wave of accomplishment washing over him.

**Megan's Quiet Approval**

Later that morning, Megan stopped by Ethan's desk, her arms crossed and an amused smile tugging at her lips.

"I heard you pulled a late one to finish the metrics report," she said.

Ethan chuckled weakly. "News travels fast around here."

Megan tilted her head. "What Noah won't say – because he's, well, Noah – is that he's impressed. He doesn't show it, but he notices when people rise to the occasion."

"Really?" Ethan asked, raising an eyebrow. "Because I kind of thought he was about to nominate me for the 'Team Liability' award yesterday."

Megan laughed. "He's tough, but he respects effort. And sprinting like that to get it done? That's effort."

Ethan let out a breath he hadn't realized he was holding. "Thanks. I guess it's nice to know he doesn't hate me."

"He doesn't hate you," Megan said. "But he'll push you until you hate him – at least a little."

Ethan grinned. "Yeah, I figured that part out."

As Megan walked away, Ethan felt a flicker of pride. For all his doubts and mistakes, he'd proved something – not just to Noah or Megan, but to himself. He could handle the pressure, he could meet the deadlines, he could rise to the occasion. He was starting to believe that maybe, just maybe, he could thrive in this environment.

**Megan and Noah: A Quiet Acknowledgment**

Later that afternoon, Megan found Noah standing by the coffee machine, staring blankly as it sputtered to life. She approached with her own mug, waiting for him to finish before speaking.

"So, Ethan pulled it off," she said casually, pouring herself a cup.

Noah didn't respond immediately. He stirred his coffee with the precision of someone measuring his words. "He did what was expected of him."

Megan smirked. "Is that your version of a compliment?"

Noah glanced at her, his expression neutral but his tone lighter than usual. "He delivered on a tight timeline. That's not nothing."

Megan raised an eyebrow. "I saw the report. It was spotless. He didn't just meet the deadline; he did it well."

Noah nodded faintly, taking a sip of his coffee. "The work was solid. He's improving. But consistency is what matters. One good sprint doesn't guarantee long-term reliability."

Megan leaned against the counter, her smirk softening into something more thoughtful. "True, but it shows he's got grit. He could've crumbled, but he didn't. That says a lot."

Noah's gaze shifted toward Ethan's desk, where the younger man was engrossed in another task, his brow furrowed in concentration.

"He's learning," Noah admitted after a moment. "But grit only gets you so far if you don't pay attention to the details. That's what I'm watching for."

"Fair enough," Megan said, her tone even. "But it wouldn't kill you to let him know he's heading in the right direction. He's still figuring out your 'tough love' management style."

Noah's lips twitched – almost a smile, but not quite. "If I start handing out praise for every decent report, I'll set a precedent I can't maintain."

Megan rolled her eyes. "God forbid people think you're human."

Noah didn't rise to the bait. Instead, he took another sip of his coffee and set the mug down. "If he keeps this up, he'll figure it out. He's not hopeless."

Megan chuckled, pushing off the counter. "Wow. High praise, coming from you."

As she walked back to her desk, she glanced over at Ethan, who was oblivious to their conversation. She allowed herself a small smile. Maybe Noah wasn't one for overt recognition, but his quiet acknowledgment spoke volumes. And for Ethan? That was a step in the right direction.

**Home Sweet Home**

Ethan stepped through the door, dropping his bag by the entryway with a heavy sigh. The sound of the television murmured faintly from the living room, but his mom's voice called out from the kitchen.

"You're on time today," she said, walking into the hallway with a dish towel slung over her shoulder. "What happened? Didn't Noah keep you late again?"

Ethan winced at the mention of his boss, running a hand through his hair as he made his way to the kitchen table. "Not tonight, but yeah, yesterday was... something."

She crossed her arms, studying him. "You were practically a zombie when you came home last night. Did all that extra effort even get noticed?"

Ethan's mind raced. He could see Noah's expression, hear his clipped tone, feel the weight of his expectations. He could feel the frustration bubbling up inside him again, the urge to push back, to defend himself. But he took a deep breath and forced himself to stay calm.

"Actually," Ethan said, leaning back in the chair, "he did acknowledge it. He said it was good work."

His mom's brow arched. "That's it? Just 'good work' after you stayed late and pulled through for him?"

"Pretty much," Ethan replied, shrugging. "But for Noah, that's like him writing me a thank-you note and throwing a parade. So... yeah, I'll take it."

His mom shook her head, sitting down across from him. "I don't know how you deal with someone like that. Doesn't he ever smile?"

Ethan smirked. "I'm starting to think he's physically incapable. I mean, I get it, though. He's just... intense. He wants everything to be perfect."

"And you think that's fair?" she asked, her voice soft but probing.

Ethan thought about it for a moment, the tension from the past two days still lingering in his shoulders. "I don't know. Maybe? It's annoying, sure, but I guess I'd rather have someone who pushes me than someone who doesn't care."

His mom nodded thoughtfully. "Still, I hope you're not letting him push you too hard. You've always been someone who does their best when they feel appreciated."

Ethan let out a dry laugh. "Well, I wouldn't say I feel appreciated, but... at least he noticed. That's something, right?"

She smiled gently, reaching over to give his hand a quick squeeze. "It is. Just don't forget that your best will always be good enough, no matter what anyone else thinks."

Ethan smiled back, the knot of stress in his chest loosening just a bit. "Thanks, Mom. I needed to hear that."

"Anytime," she said, standing and heading back toward the kitchen. "Now, how about you get that zombie look off your face before dinner? You'll scare your father."

Ethan laughed, shaking his head as he leaned back in his chair. For all the chaos at work, it was moments like these that made it easier to keep going. The warmth of his family, the unconditional love, the reminder that there was more to life than spreadsheets and deadlines – it was a lifeline, a source of strength that helped him navigate the turbulent waters of the corporate world.

CHAPTER IX

# Ethan's Creative Win

The issue reared its head during the team's midweek sync, where the vibe in the conference room was as tense as a high-stakes reality show elimination. Megan, ever the calm voice of pragmatism, stood at the front, pointing at a graph that seemed to scream, "We have a problem!" in bold, flashing neon letters.

"Our current validation process is bottlenecking the QA handoff," she said, her tone measured but laced with an undercurrent of urgency. "Manual reviews are taking too long, and that's pushing back fulfillment timelines."

The slide showed a dismal trend: delays piling up like dirty laundry in a teenager's room, threatening to engulf the entire operation.

Noah, seated at the head of the table, leaned forward, elbows on the table, his gaze sharp enough to cut glass. "What's the root cause?" he asked, his voice devoid of inflection, yet somehow conveying a sense of impending doom.

"The data," Megan replied without hesitation. "It's messy. It's not about effort—it's the sheer volume and inconsistency. It's like trying to herd cats in a hurricane."

Noah's brow furrowed, a deep crease forming between his eyes. "Fix it," he said simply, his eyes sweeping across the room like a drone scanning for targets. They finally landed on Ethan, who tried to look busy examining the table grain, hoping to blend into the wood paneling.

Ethan's heart hammered in his chest, a drumbeat of nervous energy. He could feel the weight of expectation pressing down on him, but beneath the anxiety, there was a flicker of excitement. This was his chance to prove himself, to show them what he was capable of.

He raised a hand slightly, then cleared his throat, his voice a touch shaky. "What if we automated the first pass?" he proposed, the idea taking shape in his mind as he spoke. "We could set up a system to handle basic validations and flag exceptions for manual review. It would be like a filter, catching the obvious errors and leaving the tricky ones for human eyes."

Megan frowned, her skepticism evident. "Automation sounds great in theory, but our data isn't exactly clean. An automated system could just amplify the errors instead of solving them. It's like giving a toddler a chainsaw—efficient, but potentially disastrous."

"I get that," Ethan replied quickly, trying to keep the momentum alive. "But even if we only reduce the manual workload by 20%, that's hours saved every week. It's like giving the team a superpower—the ability to see through the data clutter and focus on the real issues." He paused, his gaze meeting Noah's. "Let me take a crack at it—I'll make sure to test it thoroughly before we roll anything out. No rogue toddlers with chainsaws, I promise."

Noah's gaze was intense, unreadable. Ethan could feel himself squirming under the scrutiny, but he held his ground. Finally, after what felt like an eternity, Noah nodded.

"You have until Friday. If it doesn't work—or worse, causes chaos—we're back to manual. Understood?"

Ethan nodded, his voice barely a whisper. "Understood."

**Changing Approach**

Back at his desk, Ethan dove headfirst into a rabbit hole of online resources. He scoured forums, deciphering cryptic code snippets and jargon-filled debates. He watched YouTube tutorials, pausing and rewinding, trying to grasp the nuances of data validation and automation. He even emailed his old data analytics professor, hoping for a lifeline of guidance. The information overload was overwhelming, but he pushed through, fueled by a mix of caffeine and determination.

He spent hours sketching out flowcharts, scribbling notes on sticky notes, and building a Frankensteinian script from bits of code, forum posts, and YouTube tutorials. His desk slowly transformed into a battlefield of information, a testament to his relentless pursuit of a solution.

*"Research is exhausting," he muttered, rubbing his eyes, "but if I mess this up, Noah might actually explode. Or worse—he'll smirk."*

**Building the Solution**

The clock ticked relentlessly, each second a hammer blow against Ethan's dwindling patience. He ran test after test, his eyes glued to the screen, his fingers flying across the keyboard. The script was a Frankensteinian creation, cobbled together from bits of code, forum posts, and YouTube tutorials. It was messy, it was buggy, but it was starting to work.

He encountered roadblocks, moments of frustration where he wanted to throw his laptop out the window and join the circus. But he persevered, driven by a desire to prove himself, to show Noah and Megan that he was more than just a rookie with a knack for social media.

At one point, he realized he'd hit a wall. Begrudgingly, he grabbed his notebook and walked over to Megan's desk, his heart pounding with a mix of apprehension and hope.

"Hey," he began, notebook in hand like a shield. "Can I ask about the validation rules? I want to make sure the script mirrors what the team actually does."

Megan looked up, raising an eyebrow. "You're asking for clarification before running wild with an idea? Growth."

Ethan smirked. *"Let's call it 'lessons learned.'"*

Megan motioned for him to pull up a chair. "All right, what do you need to know?"

As she explained, Ethan jotted down notes furiously. This time, he resisted the urge to suggest changes or shortcuts. Instead, he focused on understanding the workflow exactly as it was, absorbing the nuances, the logic, the reasoning behind each step.

When he returned to his desk, the script took shape faster. Armed with Megan's insights, he fine-tuned the logic, added checks for messy data, and even built in a rollback feature just in case things went sideways. He was building not just a solution, but a safety net, a testament to his newfound understanding of the importance of accountability.

**Crunch Time**

The office was a ghost town, the empty desks and silent monitors casting long shadows in the dim light. The only sounds were the faint hum of the AC, a lonely symphony of white noise, and the rhythmic click of Ethan's keyboard, a testament to his solitary struggle.

He ran the final tests, his eyes glued to the screen, his heart pounding with a mix of anticipation and dread. The script churned through the data, its progress displayed in a series of cryptic messages and flashing lights. Ethan held his breath, his fingers hovering over the keyboard, ready to intervene at the slightest sign of trouble.

But the script held. It processed the data, flagged the errors, and completed the validation process without a hitch. Ethan exhaled slowly, a wave of relief washing over him. He had done it. He had created a solution that was both efficient and reliable, a testament to his ability to combine creativity with discipline.

He saved the file, sent himself a backup copy, and shut down his computer with a satisfied sigh. For once, the chaos felt worth it. He had pushed himself, challenged himself, and emerged victorious.

*"Let's see if this impresses the Spreadsheet Overlord,"* he muttered to himself as he grabbed his bag and headed out, a grin spreading across his face.

**Presentation Day**

Friday arrived with the relentless inevitability of a corporate deadline. Ethan found himself in the conference room, his heart pounding louder than his laptop's startup chime. Megan, Noah, and a handful of team members sat around the table, their attention focused on the projector screen where his first slide glowed in ominous blue.

"Okay," Ethan began, gripping the table edge to steady himself. "Here's what I've built."

He launched into his explanation, walking them through the system with a mix of nervous energy and determined focus. He described the logic, the checks and balances, the fallback mechanisms, his voice gaining confidence with each slide.

"The automation handles basic validations—stuff like matching formats, identifying outliers, and flagging incomplete entries. Anomalies are sent to manual review, so nothing slips through," he said, clicking to the next slide.

He showed a chart comparing traditional manual validation to his system. The results were striking: the new process shaved off 35% of the time typically spent on reviews. The team members exchanged impressed glances, their skepticism melting away.

"And here," he continued, "are the fallback mechanisms. If the script encounters something it can't confidently classify, it's flagged immediately for manual inspection. That way, we avoid any potential false negatives. It's like having a safety net for the safety net."

When he finally stopped speaking, the room fell into a weighted silence. Ethan could almost hear the buzz of the fluorescent lights overhead, a subtle reminder of the corporate world he was slowly learning to navigate.

**The Room Reacts**

Megan broke the silence first, leaning forward with a mix of curiosity and grudging respect. "It's... thorough," she admitted. "I'll be honest—I was skeptical, but the test results are promising. I'd say we pilot this for two weeks and evaluate from there."

Ethan exhaled quietly, relief flickering across his face. He had passed Megan's test, a significant hurdle in his quest for acceptance.

Noah, however, remained inscrutable. His eyes narrowed slightly as he tapped a pen against the table, a rhythmic sound that amplified the tension in the air. "How did you account for edge cases?" he asked, his tone sharp and precise.

Ethan pulled up a slide he'd prepared specifically for this question. "The system is designed to flag anything ambiguous for manual review," he explained. "I tested it with a small batch of messy data, and the fallback mechanisms caught anomalies without introducing significant delays. It's like having a backup generator for the backup generator."

Noah leaned back in his chair, studying the results on the screen. His gaze lingered on Ethan for a moment, a silent assessment that made Ethan's stomach churn. Finally, he spoke.

"It's a good start," he said, his voice calm but clipped. "But don't get complacent. Automation isn't a substitute for accountability. This system will need consistent monitoring and refinement. It's like a garden—you can't just plant the seeds and walk away. You need to tend to it, nurture it, and make sure it doesn't get overrun by weeds."

It wasn't glowing praise, but it was far from criticism. Coming from Noah, it felt like a resounding win.

**Ethan's Reaction**

Ethan stumbled out of the conference room, his legs shaky, his head spinning. The adrenaline that had fueled him through the presentation was fading, leaving behind a strange mix of relief, exhaustion, and exhilaration. He had done it. He had faced the challenge and emerged victorious. He had proven himself, not just to Noah, but to himself.

**Noah's Internal Shift**

Later that afternoon, Noah sat alone in his office, his gaze fixed on the test results Ethan had presented. His instincts told him to be cautious—automation could be a double-edged sword. Yet, he couldn't ignore the efficiency gains the system offered.

He flipped back through the slides, paying particular attention to the fallback mechanisms Ethan had outlined. They were solid. Not perfect, but solid. He had to admit, Ethan had impressed him. The kid had taken his feedback to heart, done his research, and delivered a solution that was both innovative and reliable. Maybe, just maybe, he'd underestimated Ethan.

Mila appeared in his doorway, her tumbler in hand. "So, thoughts on Ethan's latest experiment?"

Noah didn't look up immediately. "It's... functional," he said finally, his tone carefully measured.

Mila smirked, leaning against the doorframe. "Wow. That's practically a love letter coming from you."

Noah glanced up, one eyebrow raised. "He's creative," he said, setting the papers aside. "But creativity without discipline is dangerous. I need to make sure he understands that."

Mila took a sip from her tumbler, her expression thoughtful. "He's starting to. But here's the thing—you push him hard, which is good, but maybe give him a bit of breathing room to see that his ideas aren't just tolerated—they're valued. A little trust goes a long way."

Noah frowned slightly. "I trust him to improve. But I'm not going to lower my expectations. If anything, I'll raise them."

Mila grinned. "Of course, you will. Just don't forget to let him know when he's done something right. Even you have to admit, this system's a step in the right direction."

Noah didn't respond immediately, but his silence spoke volumes. Finally, he gave a small nod. "It is," he admitted.

Mila straightened, her grin widening. "There it is. Progress. You two might figure each other out yet."

As she walked away, Noah turned back to the test results, a faint trace of satisfaction flickering across his expression. He couldn't deny it – Ethan was proving to be a valuable asset to the team. He was still rough around the edges, still prone to impulsive decisions, but he was learning, adapting, and growing. And maybe, just maybe, that was enough.

**Reflection**

Ethan slumped into his chair that evening, exhausted but satisfied. Megan had already emailed him feedback on the pilot results – mostly positive, with a few cautious notes – and Noah had given him a small nod of approval as he left the office. For the first time since starting at SynergyWorks, Ethan felt like he'd genuinely contributed.

Pulling out his phone, he typed to the readers:

*Finally! A win. And hey, I even resisted the urge to wing it. Turns out, doing actual research doesn't kill you – though it might make you question your life choices.*

He paused for a moment, grinning as a new thought struck him:

*Also, shout-out to Einstein for the assist. I mean, he didn't technically help, but his whole 'insanity is doing the same thing and expecting different results' vibe really hit home today. Guess I'm not insane after all. Just a little... overly optimistic.*

He hit send on the Slack update for the team:

Workflow pilot is live! Looking forward to your feedback – please don't roast me too hard.

Across the office, Noah glanced at Ethan from his desk, catching the younger man's faint smile as he leaned back in his chair. There was still work to do, but maybe – just maybe – Ethan was starting to find his footing. And maybe, just maybe, Noah was starting to see the potential that had been there all along.

CHAPTER X

# Team Dynamics

Ethan practically bounced into the office, his grin wider than usual, his step lighter than air. He exchanged playful banter with the receptionist, his confidence radiating like a beacon. He felt invincible, like he could conquer any challenge, solve any problem, and charm his way into anyone's good graces. He winked at the security guard, who gave him a confused but slightly amused nod.

Rockstar, he thought, savoring the word. Yesterday's workflow success had him riding high, his ego inflated like a helium balloon. He could practically hear the congratulatory music playing in his head, a triumphant symphony of self-congratulation.

Sliding into his desk chair, he logged onto Slack, grinning as a few congratulatory messages lit up his screen:

Megan: Nice work on the workflow fix. Early signs look good.

Amir: Maybe you're not just the new guy after all. Good job.

Michael from HR: You're a rockstar! Don't forget to book your time in the kombucha lounge!

"*Rockstar*," Ethan muttered with a smirk, leaning back and cracking his knuckles. One win down, a million to go. He could practically see his name in lights, "*Ethan: Operations Genius*." He wondered if they gave out trophies for workflow optimization.

**The Morning Sync**

By the time the team gathered for the morning sync, Ethan's confidence was practically bouncing off the walls. He glanced around, half-listening as the others settled in, his mind already racing with ideas.

*What else can I streamline? Optimize? Revolutionize? Maybe I should pitch a company-wide nap time. Or a mandatory puppy petting break. Or a system that automatically delivers donuts to your desk every Friday.*

Noah began the meeting with his characteristic no-nonsense tone. "Today, we're focusing on cross-team collaboration," he said, his voice sharp and to the point. "Operations and Marketing have been struggling with handoffs on shared deliverables. Deadlines slip, expectations aren't aligned, and—"

"I've got an idea!" Ethan blurted out, cutting Noah off mid-sentence. The words tumbled out of his mouth before he could even process them, fueled by a potent cocktail of confidence and caffeine.

The air thickened, the room temperature dropping several degrees. Ethan could feel the weight of a dozen pairs of eyes on him, their expressions a mix of surprise, disapproval, and thinly veiled amusement. His stomach lurched, his carefully constructed confidence crumbling like a stale cookie.

All eyes turned to him, and for a split second, Ethan hesitated. The room was silent, the only sound the faint hum of the projector. He could feel his cheeks burning, his palms sweating. But then he leaned forward, determined to ride the wave of his newfound confidence, even if it was quickly turning into a tsunami of awkwardness.

"Why don't we use a centralized communication tool?" he began, his words spilling out in a rush. "Something that automates updates and makes handoffs seamless. Like a dashboard where everyone can see progress in real-time, flag issues, and reduce back-and-forth emails. It's scalable, efficient, and honestly, I can't believe we're not doing this already. It'll be like a command center for collaboration, a symphony of synchronized workflows."

He gestured as he spoke, painting a vivid picture of a futuristic, hyper-collaborative system. As the idea snowballed, his enthusiasm grew louder and faster, oblivious to the room's growing unease. He was on a roll, his mind conjuring images of sleek interfaces, flashing lights, and a team working together in perfect harmony.

When he finally stopped, he leaned back with a satisfied grin, glancing at Noah for approval. But the approval didn't come.

**The Reality Check**

Noah's gaze was like a laser beam, burning into Ethan's skin. The air crackled with tension. Ethan felt a wave of nausea wash over him. He was pretty sure he was going to throw up.

Noah didn't respond immediately. He sat still, his gaze steady, the silence stretching long enough for Ethan's grin to falter and his stomach to churn. The room was silent, the only sound the ticking of the clock on the wall, each tick a hammer blow against Ethan's dwindling confidence.

Finally, Noah spoke, his voice calm but laced with a chilling disapproval. "Ethan, did you consult anyone before pitching this?"

Ethan blinked, thrown by the question. "Uh... no. But it's a good idea. It could save us time—"

"Did you talk to Megan or anyone from Marketing to understand the specific issues they're facing?" Noah interrupted, his voice even sharper.

Ethan shifted in his seat, his earlier confidence evaporating like a puddle in the desert sun. "Not exactly, but the concept is scalable. I mean, it'd make things more efficient."

Megan's expression softened slightly, but her voice was firm, laced with a hint of warning. "The idea has potential, Ethan," she began, "but tools aren't the real problem here. The issue is what gets communicated and when. We're not struggling because we don't have enough dashboards – we're struggling because the handoff process isn't clear. It's like trying to build a house without blueprints – you might have all the tools, but you'll end up with a wonky structure."

Ethan's stomach sank. He glanced at Noah, hoping for a softer critique, a glimmer of understanding. But Noah's expression was as impassive as ever.

"Tools don't fix bad processes," Noah said, his voice a steady drumbeat of disapproval. "A dashboard might look good, but if you don't address the root problem, it's just adding another layer of complexity. Understand the issue before proposing solutions. It's like putting a bandage on a broken leg – it might look better, but it won't fix the underlying problem."

Ethan nodded quickly, his face flushed. "Got it." He wanted to disappear, to melt into the chair and become one with the conference room furniture.

Noah's gaze lingered for a moment, a silent reminder of Ethan's misstep, before he gave a curt nod. "Good. Let's move on."

As the conversation shifted, Ethan slumped back in his chair, his mind replaying the moment like a car crash in slow motion. The confidence he'd walked in with had been thoroughly dismantled, and now all he could think was: *Why didn't I just talk to Megan first? Why do I always have to learn things the hard way?*

**Noah's Subtle Shift**

As the sync wrapped up, Noah watched Ethan return to his desk, his movements slower and less self-assured than usual. Normally, Noah wouldn't give moments like this a second thought. People needed to learn from their mistakes, and sometimes, a harsh lesson was the most effective teacher.

But something about Ethan's enthusiasm stuck with him. Sure, the pitch had been off-target, a bit naive, but at least he was trying to contribute.

He wasn't afraid to speak up, to share his ideas, even if they weren't fully formed.

*Maybe I don't need to be so hard on him every time,* Noah thought, pushing his chair back from the table. He'd always believed in a sink-or-swim approach to management, but maybe there was room for a gentler touch, a bit of guidance.

He wouldn't say it out loud, but he respected effort. And Ethan? He wasn't afraid to put himself out there. That counted for something. It reminded him of himself, years ago, when he was just starting out, eager to prove himself, to make a difference.

**A Humbling Lesson**

Determined to redeem himself, Ethan spent the rest of the day gathering input. He started with Megan, who walked him through a recent project where the Operations-Marketing handoff had failed.

"It's not that we don't communicate," she explained, flipping through her notes, her voice calm and patient. "It's that what we're communicating isn't always clear or actionable. It's like trying to have a conversation in two different languages – we're both speaking, but neither of us understands what the other is saying."

She went on to explain the specific pain points: Marketing needed detailed briefs with clear objectives, target audiences, and deadlines. Operations, on the other hand, needed timely feedback and approvals to keep the projects moving.

Next, Ethan joined Marketing's team huddle under the pretense of observing, but mostly to eavesdrop. Their frustrations mirrored Megan's. One designer complained, "Operations sends over half-baked briefs, and we're left guessing. It's like they expect us to be mind-readers. By the time we align, deadlines are already slipping."

Ethan scribbled furiously, his pen racing across the page, capturing the essence of their frustrations, their pain points, their desperate pleas for clarity. He was starting to see the bigger picture, the complex web of communication that connected the teams, the subtle nuances that could make or break a project.

He even cornered Sophie in the breakroom over a quick snack. "Hey, as someone new, do you feel like the teams communicate well?"

Sophie hesitated. "Well... kinda? People are helpful, but sometimes I don't know who to ask. It's like everyone has their own way of doing things, their own language, their own secret handshake. It's a bit overwhelming."

By the time Ethan sat back at his desk, he was drained. This wasn't as simple as plugging in a new tool. He had to rethink his entire approach, to understand the underlying issues, the human element that no software could fix.

**Megan's Quiet Support**

Later in the day, Megan swung by his desk, her expression lighter than it had been during the sync. She leaned against the divider, arms crossed, a hint of amusement in her eyes.

"For what it's worth," she said, "the idea wasn't bad. Just... premature."

Ethan glanced up, surprised. "You think?"

She nodded. "Yeah. The instinct to simplify is good. But in Operations, execution matters more than ideas. It's like having a brilliant recipe – it's useless if you don't know how to cook." She paused, her expression softening. "Next time, start with understanding the pain points. Talk to people first, and then you'll have their buy-in when you pitch. It's like building a bridge – you need to start from both sides."

Ethan offered a small, sheepish grin. "Got it. Homework first, grand plans later."

Megan smirked. "You'll figure it out. Just try not to interrupt Noah again mid-sentence. That's a bold move."

Ethan laughed despite himself. "Noted."

**The Chat with Jessica**

Determined to redeem himself after his ill-fated pitch, Ethan decided to tackle the problem head-on, starting with the Marketing perspective. Jessica was the perfect person to approach – sharp, approachable, and, as he'd learned in the team sync, unafraid to call out issues.

He found her in her glass-walled office, typing with the intensity of someone trying to hit a deadline and look good doing it. Her office was a whirlwind of organized chaos, a testament to her creative energy.

"Jessica, got a second?" Ethan asked, hovering awkwardly in the doorway.

Jessica looked up, her warm smile immediately disarming. "Sure, Ethan. Come in."

Ethan stepped inside, hyper-aware of how pristine her workspace was – color-coded sticky notes lined up like soldiers, neatly stacked reports, and a framed photo of her dog wearing sunglasses. Of course, even her dog is cooler than me, he thought.

"I wanted to ask about the collaboration issues between Ops and Marketing," he began, his voice careful, his notebook open and ready. "From your side, what's the biggest challenge?"

Jessica leaned back in her chair, crossing her arms as she considered the question. "Honestly? It's the briefs we get from Operations. Sometimes they're so vague, it's like trying to assemble IKEA furniture without instructions. By the time we figure out what Ops actually wants, we're already behind schedule."

Ethan nodded, scribbling furiously in his notebook. "So it's not just timing – it's clarity?"

"Exactly," Jessica said, her tone firm but not unkind. "We don't need more tools or dashboards; we need better communication. If Ops gave us more context upfront – what the goals are, who the audience is, why it matters – it'd save us a ton of time. It's like giving us a map instead of just telling us to 'go explore.'"

Ethan felt a pang of regret, remembering his overly enthusiastic pitch about tools. "Got it," he said. "Thanks for being honest."

Jessica grinned. "Anytime. Oh, and Ethan?"

"Yeah?"

She pointed at his notebook. "Good call on taking notes. Shows you're learning."

**The Revised Plan**

Armed with insights from Jessica, Megan, and even a quick chat with Amir, Ethan sat down to rework his plan. He scrapped his overambitious ideas about tools and dashboards, focusing instead on the root problem: clarity. He realized that sometimes, the simplest solutions were the most effective.

By morning, he had a proposal he felt good about – one that wasn't just a quick fix but addressed the actual pain points he'd uncovered. It was a plan built on collaboration, on understanding, on a newfound respect for the complexities of teamwork.

During the team sync, Ethan waited until Noah opened the floor for updates. Instead of blurting out his idea, he raised his hand, heart thudding in his chest. He took a deep breath, reminding himself to stay calm, to be clear, to present his ideas with confidence and humility.

"I have a revised suggestion," he began, keeping his tone steady. "After talking to Marketing, Megan, and others, I realized the issue isn't about tools – it's about the content of our communication. I'm proposing a standard format for briefs that includes key details upfront: goals, timelines, key deliverables, and the audience. Marketing confirms expectations before starting, and we use Slack for real-time updates instead of endless email threads. It's like building a bridge – we need to make sure both sides are aligned before we start construction."

The room was silent for a beat, the only sound the soft whirring of the projector.

Megan broke the silence first, her expression shifting into a faint nod. "That's... actually a good approach. It's simple, but it addresses the core issue. It's like clearing the communication channels before sending out a message – it ensures everyone's on the same page."

A ripple of light chuckles eased the tension. Ethan glanced at Noah, whose expression was as unreadable as ever. He held his breath, waiting for the verdict.

Noah leaned back in his chair, his gaze steady. "It's a step in the right direction," he said finally. "We'll try this on the next project and assess its impact."

It wasn't effusive praise, but Ethan felt the tension in his shoulders dissolve. Coming from Noah, "a step in the right direction" was practically a gold star.

**Reflection**

That evening, Ethan sprawled on his couch, scrolling through the notes he'd made earlier. His apartment was quiet except for the faint hum of traffic outside, a welcome contrast to the day's buzzing office. He felt a sense of accomplishment, a quiet satisfaction that he had learned from his mistakes and come up with a solution that addressed the real issues.

He opened his Notes app and started typing:

*Lesson of the day: Don't rush to fix problems before understanding them. Ask questions, take notes, and talk to people who actually deal with the problem. Also, maybe don't interrupt Noah unless I have a bulletproof plan.*

He smirked and added:

*Still, a win's a win. Maybe I should start charging for these brilliant ideas.*

Satisfied, Ethan closed his phone and leaned back, a mix of humility and pride settling over him. He still had a lot to learn, but at least he was learning – and today, that felt like enough. He was starting to find his rhythm, his place in the complex symphony of SynergyWorks. He was starting to understand that success wasn't just about brilliant ideas, but about collaboration, communication, and a willingness to listen and learn.

## CHAPTER XI

# Personal Tensions

Ethan's shoulders ached, his jaw clenched, his stomach churning with a mix of anxiety and frustration. He felt like he was juggling chainsaws, each one a task, a deadline, an expectation, threatening to slip from his grasp and send his carefully constructed world crashing down around him. Noah's relentless pursuit of perfection, his unwavering focus on precision and accountability, loomed over him like a storm cloud, casting a shadow on every aspect of his life.

At home, his parents' well-meaning advice to "slow down" and "find balance" felt like a distant echo, a language from another planet. They didn't understand the pressure, the constant fear of failure, the feeling of being trapped in a never-ending race against time.

And Lauren, his girlfriend, the one person who was supposed to be his safe haven, his escape from the corporate chaos, was growing increasingly distant. Her frustration with his constant work-related stress, her longing for connection and shared experiences, was a constant reminder of his failings, another weight on his already overburdened shoulders.

Ethan felt like he was drowning, gasping for air in a sea of expectations, his own confidence eroding with every misstep, every missed deadline, every frustrated sigh from those he cared about.

**Avalanche at Work**

The office buzzed with its usual frenetic energy, a symphony of keyboards, conversations, and ringing phones. Ethan navigated the familiar maze of desks and cubicles, his footsteps heavy, his shoulders slumped. He dropped into his chair, the worn fabric offering little comfort, and stared at the daunting list of tasks that awaited him.

*"Okay, Ethan," he muttered to himself, his voice barely a whisper. "Today's the day. No more falling behind."*

But the resolve was short-lived.

"Hey, Ethan," Zara's voice cut through his thoughts, her tone all business. "Noah mentioned he's expecting the updated sales-ops projections by noon. Didn't he tell you yesterday?"

Ethan's blood ran cold. The room seemed to tilt, the spreadsheets on his screen blurring into a meaningless jumble. He could feel the panic rising in his chest, threatening to choke him.

"Uh... no, he didn't," he stammered, his voice cracking.

Zara sighed, tapping her clipboard with a brisk efficiency that mocked his own disorganization. "It's flagged as high priority. Check your tracker."

He quickly opened the project tracker, his stomach sinking as he saw the task highlighted in glaring red. It was like a beacon of failure, a spotlight on his incompetence.

"Right," he mumbled, his face burning with shame. "Thanks, Zara."

Zara gave him a tight smile, a mix of pity and disapproval, before walking off, leaving Ethan to stare at his screen in dismay. The deadline loomed, a menacing shadow cast over his already chaotic day.

**Pressure Mounts**

The clock ticked relentlessly, each second a hammer blow against Ethan's dwindling composure. He scrambled to gather the data, his fingers fumbling over the keyboard, his mind racing to catch up. The numbers swam before his eyes, blurring into a meaningless jumble. He could feel the pressure building, a suffocating weight that threatened to crush him.

By 11:30, he was barely holding it together. The draft he'd cobbled together felt rushed, incomplete, a pale imitation of the quality he knew he was capable of producing. But time was running out, the deadline looming like a guillotine.

He hit send at 11:55, his finger trembling as he clicked the button. He leaned back in his chair, his heart pounding in his chest, his breath coming in ragged gasps.

*It's enough, he told himself, his voice a desperate plea for reassurance. It has to be enough.*

But deep down, he knew it wasn't. He knew he'd cut corners, skipped steps, sacrificed quality for speed. And he knew that Noah would see right through it.

The Slack notification arrived at 12:15, a digital death knell:

Noah: "This draft is incomplete. Missing key comparisons to last quarter. We'll discuss at 2 PM."

Ethan stared at the screen, his frustration boiling over. He shoved his chair back, the screech of metal against tile echoing through the office, and stalked to the break room, his coffee cup clutched tightly in his hand. He needed an escape, a moment to breathe, to regroup, to rage against the unfairness of it all.

**Noah's Perspective**

Across the office, Noah sat at his desk, reviewing Ethan's draft. The numbers were there, but the deeper context – the comparisons, the historical insights, the narrative that gave the data meaning – was missing. It was like a skeleton without flesh, a framework without substance.

*He has potential, Noah thought, rubbing his temples, the familiar tension building behind his eyes. But potential without precision is a liability. It's like a race car without brakes – fast, but dangerous.*

He glanced at the clock. The 2 PM meeting with Ethan was coming up, and part of him dreaded it. He didn't enjoy being the hard-nosed manager, the bearer of bad news, the enforcer of standards. But years of experience had taught him that lowering standards helped no one. It was like building a house on sand – it might look good for a while, but eventually, it would crumble.

He closed the draft and leaned back in his chair, his gaze drifting towards the window. The cityscape stretched out before him, a concrete jungle teeming with ambition and struggle. He saw himself in Ethan, the young, eager employee, hungry for success, but still learning the rules of the game.

*If he's going to thrive here, Noah thought, his expression hardening with resolve, he needs to understand this isn't just about completing tasks. It's about understanding the bigger picture. It's about seeing the connections, the consequences, the ripple effects of every action. It's about accountability.*

**The Breaking Point**

Ethan entered the conference room at 2 PM with his notebook in hand, feeling like he was heading into a storm without an umbrella. Noah was already seated, laptop open, his expression calm but unreadable. The air in the room was thick with tension, the silence punctuated only by the soft hum of the air conditioning.

"Ethan," Noah began, his voice steady, each word a carefully measured weight, "let's talk about the draft you submitted. It's missing key data comparisons to last quarter. Did you review the historical trends?"

Ethan's heart sank. He could feel the blood draining from his face, his carefully constructed composure crumbling.

"I, uh... didn't have time to dig into all of it," he mumbled, his voice barely audible.

Noah's gaze hardened, his voice like ice shards. "If you didn't have time to do it thoroughly, why submit it? Speed without accuracy isn't just a mistake – it's a waste of time for everyone involved."

Ethan's frustration finally boiled over. "I'm juggling a dozen things here!" he shot back, his voice cracking with a mixture of anger and desperation. "If you want perfection, maybe stop piling everything on one person!"

Noah leaned back in his chair, crossing his arms, his expression unreadable. "If the workload feels unmanageable, it's your responsibility to communicate that. Rushing through and delivering subpar work isn't the solution."

Ethan clenched his fists under the table, his knuckles white. "I have tried communicating, but every time I do, it feels like you expect me to 'figure it out' anyway."

The room fell silent, the tension crackling in the air like static electricity. Finally, Noah spoke, his tone quieter but no less firm.

"Ethan, accountability isn't about perfection. It's about owning your responsibilities and addressing issues before they become problems. If you're overwhelmed, speak up sooner. And own the gaps – not excuse them."

Ethan nodded reluctantly, the fight draining out of him. He felt a wave of exhaustion wash over him, the weight of his mistakes pressing down on his shoulders. He knew Noah was right, but the frustration and resentment lingered, a bitter taste in his mouth.

**Clash at Home**

The familiar scent of his mom's curry usually brought a sense of comfort, a reminder of home and hearth. But tonight, it did little to soothe Ethan's frayed nerves. He pushed through the front door, his shoulders slumping as the weight of the day threatened to pull him down.

His dad was in the living room, reclined in his favorite chair, a baseball game muted on the TV. The soft hum of the commentary barely masked the quiet in the room, a quiet that mirrored the tension simmering within Ethan.

"Hey, kid," his dad called out, glancing over his shoulder.

Ethan didn't respond. He dropped his bag by the door and collapsed onto the couch, sinking so far into the cushions it felt like the room might swallow him whole.

"Long day?" his dad asked, sitting up straighter, concern etched on his face.

"Long week," Ethan muttered, staring at the ceiling, the intricate patterns of the popcorn texture suddenly fascinating. After a pause, he added, "Actually, make that a long month."

His dad muted the TV, resting his elbows on his knees as he turned to face Ethan fully. "Talk to me, son. What's going on?"

Ethan hesitated, his hands fidgeting in his lap. He wasn't used to talking about his struggles, his doubts, his fears. But something in his dad's gaze, a mix of concern and unwavering support, gave him the courage to open up.

"Work's been tough," he began, his voice barely a whisper. "Noah's been pushing me hard, and I feel like I'm barely keeping up. I messed up a deadline today, and he wasn't happy about it."

His dad nodded, his expression understanding. "It's tough starting out," he said, his voice gentle. "You're still learning the ropes, figuring out how to navigate the corporate world. It takes time."

Ethan's voice cracked as he continued, "But it's not just work. Lauren's upset because I've been neglecting her, and honestly? She's right. I don't blame her. And then there's you and Mom, always telling me to slow down, but I don't even know how to do that without feeling like I'm falling behind."

His dad's expression softened. "Ethan, you're not alone in this. We all struggle with finding balance, with juggling responsibilities, with meeting expectations. The important thing is that you're trying, that you're not giving up."

Ethan's frustration flared. "But what if trying isn't enough? What if I'm not cut out for this? What if I'm just not good enough?"

His dad's voice was firm, reassuring. "Ethan, listen to me. You're not supposed to have it all figured out yet. And anyone who tells you they did at your age is lying. The important thing is that you're learning, that you're growing, that you're not afraid to ask for help."

Ethan's defenses crumbled, tears welling up in his eyes. He hadn't cried in years, not since he was a child, but the weight of it all, the pressure, the fear, the exhaustion, was finally too much.

His dad pulled him into a hug, a silent gesture of comfort and support. Ethan clung to him, his body shaking with sobs, the tears flowing freely now, a release of pent-up emotions he hadn't even realized he was holding onto.

"It's okay," his dad murmured, his voice a soothing balm against Ethan's raw emotions. "It's okay to not be okay. We all have those moments. The important thing is to keep going, to keep learning, to keep growing."

Ethan nodded, his tears subsiding, a sense of calm settling over him. He wasn't alone. He had his family, his friends, and maybe, just maybe, he was starting to find his way in this crazy, chaotic world.

**The Call with Lauren: Rebuilding Bridges**

Later that evening, after the comforting warmth of his dad's hug and a shared meal with his family, Ethan felt a renewed sense of courage. He knew he needed to reach out to Lauren, to mend the frayed edges of their relationship, to show her that she wasn't just an afterthought, a footnote in his chaotic life.

With a deep breath, he found her name in his contacts and pressed the call button.

"Ethan," Lauren answered, her voice guarded, a hint of weariness in her tone.

"Hey," he said softly, his voice laced with a vulnerability he rarely allowed himself to show. "I just... I wanted to apologize. I haven't been the best boyfriend lately, and I'm truly sorry."

There was a long pause on the other end of the line, a silence that stretched on, filled with unspoken emotions and unanswered questions.

"I miss you," Lauren finally replied, her voice soft, a hint of sadness in her tone. "I miss spending time with you, talking to you, laughing with you. It feels like we've grown so distant lately."

Ethan's chest tightened. He knew she was right. He'd been so consumed by work, by the pressure to prove himself, that he'd neglected the one person who mattered most.

"I know," he said quickly, his voice earnest, filled with regret. "And you're right. I haven't been fair to you, and I'm sorry. I've been drowning at work, but that's not an excuse. You deserve better than that, and I want to do better."

Lauren's voice softened slightly, but there was still an edge of caution, a hint of skepticism. "I don't want to be an afterthought, Ethan. If this is going to work, I need to know you're willing to put in the effort. I need to know that I'm a priority, not just something you fit in when you have time."

"You are a priority," Ethan insisted, his voice firm, his resolve solidifying. "I talked to Noah today. Things are shifting at work, and I'm trying to get a handle on it. But more than that, I don't want to lose you, Lauren. I'll make Saturday work – no excuses."

She was quiet for a moment, the silence filled with the unspoken weight of their relationship, the fragile hope that maybe, just maybe, they could find their way back to each other.

"Okay," she finally replied, her voice a fragile whisper. "But this has to be more than just words, Ethan. I need to see it. I need to feel it."

"You will," he promised, his own voice steady, his determination unwavering. "I mean it this time."

"I want to believe you," she said, a hint of vulnerability creeping into her voice.

"You can," Ethan said, his own voice softening, a warmth spreading through him.

They talked for a few more minutes, the tension between them easing with every exchanged word. They talked about their days, their frustrations, their hopes, their fears. They talked about the things that mattered, the things that connected them, the things that reminded them why they were together in the first place.

When the call ended, Ethan felt a flicker of hope – a sense that maybe, just maybe, he could start to put the pieces back together, not just at work, but in his life as a whole.

**Mila Steps In**

The next morning, Ethan sat in the break room, staring at his coffee, the steam swirling and rising like his own confused thoughts. Mila slid into the chair across from him, her ever-present tumbler in hand, her eyes sparkling with a mix of amusement and concern.

"You look like someone canceled Christmas," she quipped, her voice a welcome intrusion into his brooding silence.

Ethan chuckled weakly, the sound hollow and brittle. "Feels like they canceled the whole year."

"What's going on?" Mila asked, her tone gentle but probing.

Ethan poured out the details – Noah's critique, his parents' comments, Lauren's frustration, the crushing weight of expectations, the fear of failure, the longing for balance. Mila listened patiently, nodding at all the right moments, her expression a mix of understanding and encouragement.

"You've got a lot on your plate," she said when he was finished, her voice calm and reassuring. "But you're not alone. We all go through this, especially when we're starting out. It's like trying to learn how to juggle while riding a unicycle on a tightrope – it's messy, it's chaotic, and it's easy to fall."

She paused, her gaze meeting Ethan's. "But you're not falling. You're learning. And learning isn't easy. It's messy, it's frustrating, and it often feels like you're taking one step forward and two steps back. But you're making progress, Ethan. You're figuring things out, and that's what matters."

Ethan's shoulders relaxed slightly, the tension easing. Mila's words were like a balm, soothing his raw emotions, reminding him that he wasn't alone in this struggle.

"Thanks, Mila," he said, his voice thick with gratitude. "I needed to hear that."

"Anytime," she said, her smile warm and genuine. "And hey, don't forget – you're not just learning the ropes at work, you're learning about yourself, about your limits, about what truly matters to you. That's a valuable lesson, even if it comes with a few bumps and bruises along the way."

Ethan nodded, a new sense of determination settling in his chest. He wasn't just an employee trying to survive in a demanding job; he was a person navigating the complexities of life, learning, growing, and evolving. And maybe, just maybe, that was the most important lesson of all.

Ethan hesitated outside Noah's office door, his hand hovering mid-air before he knocked. He hated this part—admitting vulnerability, especially to the person who seemed to embody unwavering strength and control. But Mila's words echoed in his mind: "You're learning. And learning isn't easy."

**The conversation with Noah**

He knocked lightly, the sound swallowed by the thick wooden door.

"Come in," Noah's voice called from inside, the usual crispness softened slightly, as if anticipating a conversation that wasn't purely business.

Ethan pushed the door open, stepping into the space with a mix of nervous energy and tentative resolve. Noah's office was a reflection of the man himself—orderly, efficient, and meticulously organized. Files were neatly stacked, a whiteboard displayed a strategic plan outlined in Noah's tidy handwriting, and a small bonsai tree on the windowsill looked perfectly pruned. It was a space that exuded control and purpose, a stark contrast to the chaos swirling within Ethan.

"Ethan," Noah said, setting his pen down with a deliberate click that punctuated the shift in focus. "What can I do for you?"

Ethan swallowed hard, his throat suddenly dry. "I wanted to talk about... workload," he began, his voice wobbling slightly, betraying the anxiety he was trying so hard to conceal.

Noah leaned back in his chair, his expression unreadable, but his posture inviting, motioning for Ethan to continue. He had a way of listening that made you feel seen, even if his face gave nothing away.

"I feel like I'm struggling to keep up," Ethan admitted, the words tumbling out of his mouth in a rush, a torrent of pent-up frustration and fear. "I want to deliver quality work, but there's so much on my plate that I end up rushing through things just to get them done. And I know that's not what you're looking for." He paused, his gaze meeting Noah's, searching for a sign of understanding, a glimmer of empathy.

Noah's expression softened just slightly, a subtle shift that Ethan almost missed. But it was there, a flicker of something akin to compassion in his eyes. His tone, however, remained even, controlled, professional. "Why didn't you bring this up earlier?"

Ethan hesitated, the familiar fear of judgment creeping in. "Because I didn't want to seem like I couldn't handle it. I didn't want you to think I wasn't... capable."

Noah studied him for a long moment, his gaze piercing but not unkind. It was the kind of gaze that saw through Ethan's carefully constructed facade, that recognized the fear and insecurity beneath the surface.

"Ethan," Noah said finally, his voice calm and measured, "the goal isn't to do everything—it's to do the right things well. Part of accountability is knowing when to ask for help or clarity. If you're overwhelmed, I need to hear about it before it affects your work."

Ethan nodded, a wave of relief washing over him. He wasn't alone in this. Noah wasn't just a demanding boss, a relentless taskmaster; he was also a mentor, a guide, someone who wanted him to succeed.

"So... can we go over priorities? Figure out what's most important?" Ethan asked, his voice gaining confidence.

Noah pulled up Ethan's task list on his laptop, scrolling through the assignments, his brow furrowed in concentration. "We'll reallocate some of these to the team. Focus on the projections and the QA review for now. I'll adjust the deadlines for the other tasks."

Ethan blinked, surprised. "Wait—you'll adjust them?"

Noah smirked faintly, a rare sight that almost made Ethan laugh. "You think I like setting people up to fail? My job is to make sure you succeed, not burn out. But I can't help if you don't communicate."

The tension in Ethan's chest loosened. "Thanks, Noah. I'll make sure to speak up sooner next time."

Noah gave a short nod. "Good. And one more thing—precision matters, Ethan. If you want to innovate, that's fine, but it has to be built on a foundation of trust and accountability. Remember that."

Ethan left the office feeling lighter, though Noah's words about trust lingered. He wasn't sure he'd fully earned that yet, but at least he had a clearer path forward. He had a mentor, a guide, and a renewed sense of purpose.

CHAPTER XII

# Noah's Perspective

The coffee pot hissed softly in Noah's kitchen, the aroma of freshly brewed Colombian roast mingling with the lingering scent of pine cleaner. He leaned against the cool granite countertop, the warmth of the mug seeping into his palms, a comforting contrast to the chill that clung to the February air. He stirred his coffee absentmindedly, the rhythmic clinking of the spoon against ceramic a soothing counterpoint to the whirlwind of thoughts and emotions swirling within him.

His gaze drifted towards the window, drawn to the soft glow of the cityscape in the distance. The city lights twinkled like a constellation of ambition and dreams, a stark contrast to the quiet solitude of his kitchen. But it was the framed photo perched on the windowsill that truly captured his attention, a snapshot frozen in time, a portal to a past that felt both distant and intimately familiar.

The photo was a faded relic from his college days, a picture of a much younger version of himself, flanked by two of his closest friends and roommates. They were standing outside a cramped, nondescript office building, their ill-fitting suits and awkward grins a testament to their youthful naiveté and boundless optimism. The year was 2009, a time when the world felt full of promise, a time before the ground crumbled beneath their feet, before the dreams they'd nurtured for so long were shattered by the harsh realities of a global economic crisis.

Noah's grip on the coffee mug tightened, his knuckles white, the ceramic pressing against his skin a physical manifestation of the tension coiling within him. The memories surfaced like a tidal wave, washing over him, bringing with them the familiar sting of fear, the gnawing uncertainty, the relentless pressure that had shaped his early years.

He could almost taste the bitterness of those days, the metallic tang of fear mingling with the stale flavor of instant ramen noodles. He could almost feel the chill of those long winter nights, the biting wind seeping through the cracks in their drafty apartment, the threadbare blankets offering little solace against the cold. He could almost hear the echo of their anxieties, the whispered fears about the future, the doubts that gnawed at their confidence, the frustration that simmered beneath the surface of their forced optimism.

He remembered the endless stream of rejection letters, each one a paper cut to his soul, a reminder of his perceived inadequacy. He remembered the soul-crushing interviews, the thinly veiled pity in the eyes of the interviewers, the polite dismissals that chipped away at his self-worth. He remembered the dwindling bank account, the numbers shrinking with alarming speed, a constant reminder of the precariousness of their situation.

He remembered the cramped apartment they shared, the three of them crammed into a space meant for one, their personal belongings overflowing from every corner, their dreams and aspirations vying for space in the suffocating reality of their circumstances. He remembered the leaky faucets, the peeling paint, the creaking floorboards that whispered tales of past tenants and forgotten dreams. He remembered the constant threat of eviction, the fear that hung over them like a sword of Damocles, ready to sever the fragile thread that held their lives together.

He remembered the nights spent hunched over spreadsheets in the dimly lit living room, the flickering fluorescent light casting long shadows on their tired faces, the only sounds the rhythmic tapping of keyboards and the occasional frustrated sigh. They were soldiers in a silent war, battling against an invisible enemy, their weapons the spreadsheets and financial reports that held the key to their survival.

He remembered the hunger, the gnawing emptiness in his stomach that no amount of ramen noodles could satisfy. He remembered the nights when they would pool their meager resources to buy a single pizza, dividing it into thirds with mathematical precision, each slice a symbol of their shared struggle, their shared determination to survive.

He remembered the cold, the biting winter wind that seeped through the cracks in the windows, the threadbare blankets that offered little warmth. He remembered huddling together on the couch, sharing body heat and whispered jokes, trying to find solace in their camaraderie, their shared defiance against the harsh realities of the world.

He remembered the fear, the constant worry that the next paycheck wouldn't come, that the lights would be cut off, that they would be forced to abandon their dreams and return to their parents' homes in defeat. He remembered the sleepless nights, the tossing and turning, the nightmares that haunted his waking hours, the anxieties that gnawed at his soul.

Noah closed his eyes, the memories swirling and merging, a kaleidoscope of anxieties and frustrations, of triumphs and defeats. He had survived those years, had emerged from the crucible of the Great Recession stronger, more resilient, more determined. But the scars remained, a testament to the battles fought and the lessons learned.

He had learned the value of hard work, the importance of perseverance, the necessity of attention to detail. He had learned that in a world where nothing was guaranteed, where the ground could shift beneath your feet at any moment, precision and accountability were not just desirable qualities, but essential survival skills. They were the tools that had kept him afloat, the weapons that had helped him fight his way out of the abyss.

He had learned to distrust shortcuts, to value process over improvisation, to prioritize reliability over flair. He had learned to be the steady hand, the calm voice in the storm, the one who could be counted on to get the job done, no matter the obstacles. He had learned to be the rock, the anchor, the one who would never let his team down.

And he had learned to be wary of those who hadn't faced the same challenges, who hadn't tasted the bitterness of defeat, who hadn't felt the sting of failure. He saw in them a naiveté, a lack of appreciation for the fragility of success, a tendency to take things for granted. He saw in them a reflection of his younger self, the one who had once believed that the world was his oyster, that success was inevitable, that the future was secure.

He saw in Ethan a reflection of that younger self, the eager enthusiasm, the thirst for innovation, the impatience with the mundane. But he also saw the potential for recklessness, the tendency to cut corners, the lack of understanding of the consequences that could ripple outward from a single misstep.

Noah opened his eyes, his gaze hardening with resolve. He wouldn't let Ethan make the same mistakes he had. He would push him, challenge him, force him to confront his own limitations, to understand the value of discipline, the importance of accountability. He would be the mentor he wished he'd had, the guide who would lead Ethan through the turbulent waters of the corporate world, the one who would help him navigate the challenges, overcome the obstacles, and emerge stronger, more resilient, more capable.

He would be the one to teach Ethan that in a world where the only constant was change, the only way to survive was to adapt, to learn, to grow. And he would do it, not by coddling him, but by pushing him, by challenging him, by holding him to a standard that Ethan might not yet understand, but would one day appreciate.

**Team Dynamics at Noah's Home**

By the time Friday evening rolled around, Noah's house was buzzing with a different kind of energy, a more relaxed and convivial atmosphere than the usual sterile environment of the office. The aroma of baked lasagna, his signature dish for team gatherings, a comforting blend of Italian spices and melted cheese, filled the air, mingling with the sounds of laughter and conversation, creating a symphony of warmth and camaraderie.

Ethan arrived last, a store-bought dessert clutched awkwardly in his hands, his expression a mix of apprehension and eagerness. He looked like a schoolboy at his first dance, unsure of the steps, yet eager to join the fun. "Uh, hey, Noah," he mumbled, hovering near the door, his usual confidence faltering in the face of this unfamiliar social setting. "Thanks for inviting us."

Noah gave a small nod, his expression softening slightly. "Thanks for coming. You can set that on the counter."

As Ethan wandered off to join the others, Noah observed him from a distance, his gaze analytical, assessing. He saw the awkwardness, the uncertainty, but also the genuine desire to connect, to be part of the team. He saw the potential for growth, the spark of something special that could be nurtured and developed.

The group had split into smaller pockets, each conversation a microcosm of the team dynamics that Noah had carefully cultivated. Zara and Jessica were engaged in a lively debate about marketing strategies, their voices animated and passionate, their ideas bouncing off each other like volleyballs in a heated match. Megan and Mila were sharing a quiet laugh over an inside joke, their camaraderie evident in their easy smiles and comfortable silences. Amir and Sophie were playfully arguing over which snacks to claim, their banter lighthearted and teasing, a testament to the bonds they had formed.

For a moment, Noah stood on the outskirts, observing the scene, a sense of quiet satisfaction settling over him. This was his team, a diverse group of individuals with unique strengths and perspectives, each contributing to the success of the whole. It was his responsibility to nurture their talents, to guide their growth, to create an environment where they could thrive, where they could push each other to be their best, where they could support each other through challenges and celebrate each other's successes.

He wasn't just a manager, a taskmaster, an enforcer of rules. He was a leader, a mentor, a guardian of their potential. And as he watched them interact, laugh, and connect, he felt a flicker of pride, a sense of purpose that transcended the spreadsheets and deadlines that usually consumed his days. He saw in them a reflection of his own journey, the struggles, the triumphs, the lessons learned, and the bonds forged. And he knew that he was exactly where he was supposed to be.

CHAPTER XIII

# Noah's Perspective Continued

The quiet hum of the dishwasher filled the silence that had settled between Noah and Ethan. It was a comfortable silence, a space for reflection and contemplation, a stark contrast to the usual frenetic energy of the office.

Noah wasn't one for small talk, for idle chatter that filled the air but held little substance. He preferred the language of action, of results, of tangible progress. But as he glanced at Ethan, he noticed something different, a shift in the younger man's demeanor that drew his attention. Maybe it was the way Ethan carefully set down each dish, his movements deliberate and methodical, a stark contrast to his usual impulsive energy. Or maybe it was the absence of his usual quips and jokes, the silence that spoke volumes about the weight he was carrying. Whatever it was, it tugged at Noah's awareness, a subtle dissonance that disrupted the usual rhythm of their interactions.

"You doing okay, Ethan?" Noah asked finally, his voice softer than usual, a hint of concern seeping through his typically stoic facade. He leaned back against the counter, his arms crossed, his posture relaxed, yet his gaze intense, focused on Ethan's face, searching for clues to the turmoil brewing beneath the surface.

Ethan hesitated, his shoulders slumping slightly, as if the weight of the question was a physical burden. "I don't know, to be honest," he admitted, his voice barely a whisper, the words heavy with unspoken anxieties. "Everything feels like... a lot lately."

Noah nodded, his expression unreadable, but his eyes conveying a quiet understanding. "Workload getting to you?" he asked, the question hanging in the air, inviting Ethan to open up, to share the burdens that were weighing him down.

Ethan nodded, his gaze dropping to the floor, the intricate patterns of the tile suddenly fascinating. "Work, life, everything," he mumbled, his voice thick with emotion. "I mean, I want to do well here, but sometimes it feels like I'm drowning, and no one's throwing me a life preserver. It's like I'm constantly treading water, barely keeping my head above the surface, and the waves just keep coming, relentless and unforgiving."

He paused, his gaze meeting Noah's, a flicker of vulnerability in his eyes. "And then I think about you – how you seem to handle it all without breaking a sweat – and it just makes me feel... inadequate, I guess."

A flicker of something akin to warmth crossed Noah's face, a subtle softening of his usually stern features. It was a fleeting moment, easily missed, but it was there, a hint of vulnerability, a glimpse of the human being beneath the armor of the demanding manager.

"Ethan," he said finally, his voice steady, a calming presence in the midst of Ethan's swirling emotions, "you ever hear the phrase, 'Smooth seas don't make skilled sailors'?"

Ethan gave a faint smile, a glimmer of recognition in his eyes. "Yeah. It's one of those motivational poster things, right? Like the ones in the office?"

Noah chuckled softly, shaking his head. "Yeah, it sounds cheesy, but there's truth to it. Let me tell you something about my own stormy seas."

**Noah's Story: The Great Recession**

Noah motioned for Ethan to sit down at the kitchen table, his gesture inviting, welcoming. He pulled out a chair across from him, clasping his hands together as if bracing himself for what he was about to share, the memories he had kept locked away for so long, the vulnerabilities he rarely allowed himself to acknowledge.

"When I graduated in 2009," Noah began, his voice low, measured, each word carrying the weight of experience, "the job market wasn't just tough—it was brutal. I majored in business, thought I had it all figured out. I had this image of myself, you know, climbing the corporate ladder, making a difference, securing my future. But then the Great Recession hit, and everything changed overnight. The world I thought I knew, the world I thought I was prepared for, vanished. It was like stepping off a cliff and realizing there was no ground beneath my feet."

Ethan leaned forward slightly, his curiosity piqued, his own anxieties momentarily forgotten as he was drawn into Noah's story.

"My first job was an unpaid internship at a financial firm," Noah continued, his tone turning reflective, the memories swirling and resurfacing, painting a vivid picture of a time of struggle and uncertainty. "It wasn't glamorous. I'd commute two hours each way to sit in a cubicle and do grunt work—data entry, filing, fetching coffee. Half the time, I wondered if anyone even knew I was there. I felt like a ghost, a shadow, invisible in the grand scheme of things."

"Two hours?" Ethan asked, his eyebrows raising, a flicker of disbelief in his eyes.

Noah nodded. "Two hours each way. On a good day, with no delays. I was living with two roommates in a tiny apartment, and between rent, student loans, and trying to keep the lights on, there wasn't much left over. We'd split dollar-menu meals some nights, just to make it through the week. Ramen noodles were a luxury, a gourmet feast compared to some of the things we ate."

Ethan blinked, the weight of the story beginning to sink in. He'd heard about the recession, of course, but it had always felt distant, abstract, something that happened to other people, not to someone like Noah, someone who exuded competence and control.

**The Cost of Survival**

"There was no room for mistakes back then," Noah said, his voice hardening, the memories of those desperate days etching themselves onto his face, the lines around his eyes deepening, his jaw clenching. "One slip-up could mean losing that internship, and without a job lined up after, I was screwed. I worked nights as a barista just to cover my train fare. I'd be up at 4 AM, pouring coffee for people who looked down on me, then heading straight to the office, trying to pretend like I wasn't dead on my feet."

Ethan winced. "That... sounds awful," he mumbled, his own complaints about workload and deadlines suddenly seeming trivial in comparison.

"It was," Noah admitted, his voice raw with emotion. "But it taught me something: precision matters. Reliability matters. If I didn't get it right the first time, there wasn't going to be a second chance. I learned how to pay attention to every detail because my survival depended on it. It wasn't just about getting the job done; it was about proving my worth, showing them that I was valuable, that I deserved to be there."

He paused, staring down at his hands, the lines and calluses a testament to the years of hard work, the battles fought and won. "When you've lived through that kind of pressure, it sticks with you. You start to see every mistake as a potential disaster. That's why I'm hard on you, Ethan. I push because I know what it's like to work with no safety net. And even though you're not in the same position I was, I want you to understand the value of discipline. It's not about making your life hard—it's about preparing you for when things get hard. It's about building resilience, the kind of resilience that will help you weather any storm."

**Ethan's Response**

Ethan leaned back in his chair, his expression thoughtful, his eyes wide with a newfound understanding. He'd never seen this side of Noah before, the vulnerability, the raw emotion, the glimpse behind the curtain of the stoic manager. It was a revelation, a shift in perspective that changed the way he saw not just Noah, but the world itself.

"I guess I never really thought about it that way," he admitted, his voice soft, humbled. "I mean, I knew the recession was bad, but I didn't realize how personal it was for people like you. I didn't realize the sacrifices you made, the struggles you faced, the sheer determination it took to survive."

Noah gave a small nod, a flicker of gratitude in his eyes. "Most people your age didn't see it firsthand. And that's a good thing, honestly. But it also means you might not fully understand why someone like me values accountability and precision so much. It's not just about work – it's about resilience. It's about building a foundation that can withstand anything life throws at you."

Ethan hesitated before speaking, his mind racing, trying to process the implications of Noah's story, the connection he was starting to feel with this man who had always seemed so distant, so intimidating. "I guess... I've been looking at it all wrong. I thought you were just being overly critical because you didn't trust me. But maybe it's more than that. Maybe it's about wanting me to be prepared, to be resilient, to be able to handle whatever comes my way."

"It is," Noah said quietly, his voice filled with a sincerity that surprised Ethan.

**The Takeaway**

A comfortable silence settled between them, a shared understanding that transcended words. The air crackled with a newfound connection, a bridge built between two generations, two perspectives, two individuals who were finally starting to see each other, not just as boss and employee, but as human beings.

"You know," Ethan said finally, breaking the silence with a tentative smile, "this is the longest conversation we've ever had that didn't involve you telling me to fix something."

Noah smirked, the faintest hint of warmth in his expression, a rare sight that made Ethan's heart lift. "Don't get used to it," he said, his voice dry, but the underlying humor unmistakable.

Ethan laughed, the tension easing slightly, the weight on his shoulders lessening. "Noted. But... thanks for sharing all that. It helps. Really."

Noah stood, grabbing their empty glasses and placing them in the sink, his movements deliberate but unhurried. "Just don't let it go to your head, Einstein. You've got potential, but potential doesn't mean much without action. It's like having a toolbox full of tools – they're useless if you don't know how to use them."

"Got it, boss," Ethan said, standing as well, a newfound confidence in his voice. "And for the record, I'm starting to think you're not as scary as everyone says."

"Keep that to yourself," Noah said dryly. "I've got a reputation to maintain."

As Ethan walked toward the door, he paused and turned back, a genuine smile spreading across his face. "Noah?"

"Yeah?"

"Thanks. For everything."

Noah nodded, his expression unreadable, but his eyes conveying a message that Ethan couldn't quite decipher, a mix of acknowledgment, encouragement, and maybe even a hint of pride.

"Goodnight, Ethan. See you Monday."

Ethan stepped out into the cool night air, the city lights twinkling like a promise of possibilities. He had a lot to learn, a lot of challenges to face, but he wasn't alone. He had Noah, he had Mila, he had his family, and he had a newfound understanding of the man who had once seemed so distant, so intimidating. And as he walked towards home, he felt a sense of hope, a belief that maybe, just maybe, he could navigate the stormy seas and find his own path to success.

CHAPTER XIV

# Ethan's First Team Task

Ethan's pulse quickened, his palms sweating. He could feel the weight of Noah's gaze on him, a silent expectation that made his stomach churn. He gripped his pen tightly, the smooth metal a comforting anchor in the storm of his anxiety.

"Ethan, you'll be coordinating the data flow updates for this project," Noah announced, his voice cutting through the usual hum of the weekly team sync. It wasn't a question, it wasn't a suggestion, it was a directive, a challenge issued with the unwavering authority that Noah exuded.

"Got it," Ethan responded, his voice a touch too high, betraying the nervousness he was trying so hard to conceal. He scribbled the task onto his notepad, the pen digging into the paper, a physical manifestation of the pressure he felt building within him.

Noah's gaze didn't waver, his eyes boring into Ethan, assessing his reaction, gauging his readiness. "Remember, this isn't a solo mission. Delegate effectively, set clear expectations, and follow up. The team's relying on you."

Ethan nodded quickly, his mind already racing, trying to process the implications of this new responsibility. Delegate, expectations, follow up. The words echoed in his mind, a mantra of leadership, a framework for success. Easy enough, right? he thought, a flicker of doubt creeping into his confidence.

By the time the meeting ended, Ethan's mind was a whirlwind of tasks, deadlines, and potential pitfalls. He could feel the pressure mounting, the responsibility weighing heavily on his shoulders. He had to get this right, not just for himself, but for the team, for the project, for Noah.

**The Planning Phase**

Ethan gathered his sub-team – Zara, Megan, and Amir – in a quiet corner of the office, their faces a mix of curiosity and anticipation. He took a deep breath, trying to project an air of calm confidence, though his insides felt like a swarm of bees.

"Okay, here's the deal," he began, his voice a touch shaky, but gaining strength as he laid out the plan. "We need to update the data flows for the new CRM integration. Noah's expecting progress by Friday, so we'll need to move fast. It's like a relay race – we each have our part to play, and we need to pass the baton smoothly to reach the finish line."

Zara raised an eyebrow, her expression a mix of skepticism and challenge. "Do you have a breakdown of tasks?" she asked, her voice sharp, her gaze piercing.

"Uh, not yet," Ethan admitted, his cheeks flushing slightly. "But I'll sort that out tonight and send you all an email. I'll create a detailed plan, with clear deadlines and responsibilities. Think of it as a roadmap to success."

Megan exchanged a glance with Zara, a silent communication that Ethan couldn't quite decipher, but it made his stomach churn. Amir, however, nodded, his expression calm and reassuring. "Just let us know where you need us," he said, his voice steady, a calming presence in the midst of Ethan's growing anxiety.

Ethan smiled, grateful for Amir's laid-back attitude, a welcome contrast to the tension he felt radiating from Zara and Megan. "Will do. Thanks, team!" he said, his voice regaining its confidence. He would prove them wrong, show them that he was capable of leading, of delegating, of delivering results.

**Overcommitting**

That night, Ethan sat at his desk, the office lights dimmed, the only sounds the hum of the air conditioning and the rhythmic tapping of his keyboard. A half-empty coffee mug sat beside him, the lukewarm liquid a testament to the hours he'd spent hunched over his laptop, wrestling with the task ahead. His initial plan to divide the work evenly had dissolved as doubts crept in, insidious and persistent.

What if they don't get it done on time? What if it's not up to Noah's standards? What if I fail? The questions gnawed at him, fueling his anxiety, pushing him towards a familiar pattern of overcompensation.

He started assigning himself the lion's share of the tasks, reasoning that it was just easier to do it himself. He knew the data, he understood the systems, he could ensure the quality. Why risk delegating to others when he could control the outcome?

By the next morning, his to-do list was a mile long, a daunting testament to his self-imposed burden. He sent the team vague instructions, keeping the bulk of the work on his plate, his emails a carefully crafted facade of delegation that masked his underlying fear of failure.

**The Midweek Crunch**

By Wednesday, Ethan was drowning. He'd underestimated how much time the updates would take, and his Slack channels were flooded with messages from Zara and Megan, their polite requests for clarification masking a growing frustration that Ethan could sense even through the digital medium.

"Ethan," Zara's voice cut through the office hum, her tone sharp, her expression a mix of annoyance and concern. "I've been trying to figure out your notes, but they're a bit... scattered. Can you clarify what I'm supposed to be working on?"

Ethan looked up, his stress evident in the dark circles under his eyes, the tension in his shoulders, the way his fingers fidgeted with the pen in his hand. "I—yeah, sorry," he stammered, his voice betraying his exhaustion. "I've just been trying to handle the tricky parts myself, and I guess I didn't explain things clearly."

Megan, who had overheard the conversation, stepped in, her voice calm but firm. "Ethan, delegation isn't about offloading the easy stuff. It's about trusting your team to handle the work they're assigned. If you try to do everything yourself, you'll burn out – and the project will suffer."

Ethan opened his mouth to defend himself, to justify his actions, but the words wouldn't come. He knew she was right. He'd fallen into a familiar trap, the trap of believing that he could do it all himself, that he was the only one capable of meeting Noah's exacting standards.

**Megan's Advice**

Later that afternoon, Megan pulled Ethan aside, her expression softer now, a hint of understanding in her eyes. She led him to a quiet corner of the office, away from the prying eyes and ears of their colleagues.

"Look, I get it," she began, her voice gentle but firm. "You're trying to make sure everything goes smoothly, and you want to impress Noah. But leading isn't about being a one-person army. It's about collaboration. It's about trusting your team, leveraging their strengths, and working together to achieve a common goal."

Ethan sighed, the weight of his mistakes settling heavily on his shoulders. "I just... I don't want to let anyone down. I don't want to fail."

Megan crossed her arms, her expression softening further. "That's exactly why you need to trust the team. Zara's great with data mapping, and Amir's solid with testing integrations. Use their strengths. Give them the opportunity to shine. And remember – clear communication is key. If they don't know what you need, they can't deliver. It's like trying to build a house without blueprints – you'll end up with a wonky structure."

Ethan nodded slowly, the truth of her words sinking in. "You're right. I've been so focused on doing it all myself that I've barely given them a chance. I've been so afraid of failure that I've robbed them of the opportunity to succeed."

Megan smiled, a genuine smile that reached her eyes. "Lesson learned, then. Now go fix it."

**Course Correction**

The next day, Ethan gathered the team, his heart pounding with a mix of apprehension and determination. He stood before them, not as a leader dictating orders, but as a collaborator seeking their help, their expertise, their trust.

"Hey, everyone," he began, his voice humble, his gaze meeting each of theirs in turn. "So, I owe you an apology. I've been trying to take on too much instead of trusting you to do what you're great at. That changes now. I realize I haven't been the best leader, but I'm learning, and I'm hoping you'll give me another chance."

He laid out a clearer plan, assigning specific tasks based on each person's strengths. He gave Zara the data mapping, trusting her meticulous attention to detail. He gave Amir the integration testing, knowing his methodical approach would ensure thoroughness. And he kept a portion of the work for himself, the tasks that played to his own strengths, his creativity, and his problem-solving skills.

Zara's relief was evident as she dove into her part of the project, her eyes lighting up with a familiar spark of enthusiasm. Amir gave Ethan a thumbs-up, a silent gesture of support and encouragement. And Megan, observing from a distance, allowed herself a small smile. Ethan was learning, growing, evolving. He was becoming a leader.

By Friday, the updates were completed and tested, the team working together seamlessly, their individual strengths complementing each other, their communication clear and efficient. The presentation to Noah went smoothly, with Zara and Amir stepping up to explain their contributions, their voices confident and assured.

**Noah's Reaction**

After the meeting, Noah caught Ethan in the hallway, his expression unreadable, but his tone softer than usual. "Good work, Ethan," he said, his words carrying a weight of approval that Ethan hadn't expected. "The team delivered."

Ethan blinked, startled by the rare compliment. "Thanks," he mumbled, his cheeks flushing slightly. "I, uh, couldn't have done it without them."

Noah gave a small nod, a subtle gesture of acknowledgment. "That's the point. Keep it up."

As Noah walked away, Ethan couldn't help but grin. He'd done it. He'd led the team, he'd delegated effectively, he'd delivered results. And he'd earned Noah's approval, a validation that felt more rewarding than any trophy or bonus.

**Reflection**

Later that evening, Ethan flopped onto his couch, the exhaustion of the week catching up with him. But beneath the fatigue, there was a sense of accomplishment, a quiet satisfaction that he had faced the challenge and emerged victorious. He had learned a valuable lesson about leadership, about teamwork, about trusting others and empowering them to shine.

He pulled out his phone, his fingers flying across the screen as he typed a message to his unseen audience:

Okay, so maybe being the boss isn't just barking orders and looking cool. Turns out, you actually have to trust people and, you know, communicate. Who knew? It's like conducting an orchestra – you need to know when to lead, when to follow, and when to let each instrument shine.

He paused for a moment, grinning as a new thought struck him:

Anyway, baby steps. Next stop, world domination – after a nap.

He chuckled to himself, closing his eyes, the image of a world ruled by spreadsheets and data-driven decisions dancing in his head. He was still learning, still growing, but he was on the right track. And that, he realized, was the most satisfying feeling of all.

## CHAPTER XV

# Office Politics Unveiled

Ethan's stomach churned, a knot of frustration tightening in his chest. The air in the office crackled with a tension thicker than the pre-meeting coffee, and the usual camaraderie had been replaced by an undercurrent of suspicion and resentment. Ethan could practically taste the bitterness in the air, a potent cocktail of disappointment and simmering ambition.

The promotion announcements had been made that morning, and the fallout was spectacular. He wasn't up for a promotion himself—he hadn't been at SynergyWorks long enough—but he watched the reactions unfold around him like a slow-motion train wreck. Some people wore the strained smiles of those who'd dodged a bullet, while others were frozen in a state of disbelief, their dreams of career advancement lying in shattered pieces on the floor.

Then came the whispers, the hushed conversations that snaked through the office like tendrils of discontent, each word a venomous barb aimed at the perceived injustice of it all.

"You've got to be kidding me," someone muttered near the coffee machine, their voice laced with disbelief and indignation. "I thought Priya was a lock for that role. She practically carried the team on her back for the last six months."

"Nope," another voice responded, a hint of malicious glee in their tone. "Guess who got it? Brian."

Ethan's eyebrows shot up, his disbelief morphing into a slow burn of anger. Brian? Promoted? The guy who spent more time curating his LinkedIn profile than actually contributing to the team? The guy who was always mysteriously absent during crunch time, only to reappear just in time to take credit for the team's successes? It was a slap in the face to everyone who had actually put in the work, who had sacrificed their evenings and weekends to meet deadlines and deliver results.

Ethan couldn't contain his frustration any longer. He had to vent, to share his outrage with someone who would understand. He found Mila in the printing room, her ever-present tumbler in hand, waiting for the printer to spit out a document at its usual glacial pace.

"I don't get it," he admitted, shaking his head, his voice laced with a mixture of confusion and anger. "Priya practically ran that last project. How does Brian end up with the promotion?"

Mila's smirk was a mixture of amusement and sympathy. She'd seen it all before, the naive idealism of newcomers crashing against the harsh realities of the corporate world. "Ah," she said, her voice laced with a hint of irony, "you've hit the unspoken wall of corporate life. The wall where hard work meets office politics."

Ethan crossed his arms, his frustration simmering. "I thought promotions were based on performance. On results. On merit."

Mila chuckled, a dry, humorless sound. "Bless your heart, rookie. Look, performance matters. But visibility? That's what seals the deal. It's not enough to just do the work; you have to make sure the right people see you doing the work. It's like a tree falling in the forest – if no one's around to hear it, does it make a sound?"

Ethan frowned, his mind grappling with this new reality. "So... you're saying I should stop focusing on doing my job and start—what? Schmoozing? Playing politics? Kissing up to the boss?"

Mila sighed, her patience wearing thin. "No, rookie. I'm saying you need to start treating your work like it's something people need to know about. You can't assume great work speaks for itself. If no one hears it, it's like a podcast with zero listeners. You need to find a way to amplify your accomplishments, to make sure your contributions are recognized, to build relationships with the people who matter."

Ethan's mind reeled. Was this what it took to succeed in the corporate world? To play the game, to schmooze and strategize, to make sure your name was always on everyone's lips, even if it meant sacrificing integrity and authenticity?

That night, at a company mixer, he spotted Sophie across the room, her familiar smirk a beacon in the sea of unfamiliar faces. He navigated the crowd, dodging awkward conversations and lukewarm hors d'oeuvres, until he reached her side.

"You look like someone just found out their salary is public info," she teased, her eyes twinkling with amusement.

Ethan exhaled, the weight of his realization settling heavily on his shoulders. "Worse. Just realized that working hard isn't enough. It's like trying to win a race with your shoelaces tied together – you might be fast, but you're not going to get very far."

Sophie's smirk widened, a knowing glint in her eyes. "Mila gave you the 'visibility matters' speech, huh?"

"You've heard it before?"

"Heard it? Honey, I've lived it," she admitted, her voice taking on a serious tone. "Early on, I figured if I nailed my projects, people would notice. Turns out, people are too busy juggling their own to-do lists and anxieties to notice unless you remind them. So now, I make sure my work is impossible to ignore – whether that's updating leadership, speaking up in meetings, or just making sure credit is given where it's due. It's like marketing your own personal brand – you have to showcase your value, your accomplishments, your unique contributions to the team."

Ethan took a slow sip of his lukewarm beer, the bitterness mirroring his own feelings. Was this what it meant to be an adult, to play the game, to sacrifice your ideals for the sake of climbing the corporate ladder?

He looked around the room, the faces of his colleagues blurring into a sea of ambition and competition. He saw the subtle nods, the whispered conversations, the carefully cultivated alliances. He saw the game being played, the unspoken rules that governed success and failure. And he realized that if he wanted to thrive in this environment, he had to learn how to play the game, too.

But he would play it his own way, with integrity and authenticity, with a focus on collaboration and mutual respect. He would find a way to balance his idealism with the realities of the corporate world, to be both successful and true to himself. He would learn the rules, master the game, and then, maybe, just maybe, he would change the rules altogether.

**Noah's Observation**

Across the room, Noah observed Ethan deep in conversation with Sophie, their heads bent close together, their expressions animated. He couldn't hear what they were saying, but he could sense the intensity of their exchange, the spark of connection that resonated between them.

He's got a good head on his shoulders, that kid, Noah thought, a rare flicker of approval warming his usually stoic features. He's still learning the ropes, but he's got the right instincts. He's not afraid to ask questions, to challenge the status quo, to push for better ways of doing things.

Noah had always valued those qualities, even if he didn't always show it. He'd seen too many people get complacent, settle into the comfortable routines, accept the way things were without questioning, without striving for improvement. Ethan, on the other hand, had a fire in him, a drive that reminded Noah of his younger self, the one who had dared to dream, to challenge, to innovate.

He watched as Ethan excused himself from the conversation and headed towards the bar, his shoulders squared, his step purposeful.

He's got a long way to go, Noah thought, his expression hardening slightly. But he's got the potential to be great. If he can learn to temper his impulsiveness with discipline, to balance his creativity with accountability, he could become a force to be reckoned with.

A flicker of a smile touched Noah's lips, a rare sight that would have surprised his team. He was starting to see something special in Ethan, a spark that could ignite a fire, a potential that could reshape the future of Operations. And for the first time, he felt a twinge of excitement, a sense of anticipation for what the future held, for the journey they would take together, for the lessons they would learn from each other.

CHAPTER XVI

# Validation, Vulnerability, and Vision

The glow of the monitor reflected in Ethan's eyes, the lines of code blurring into a hypnotic dance of logic and precision. He'd been working for hours, fueled by a potent cocktail of caffeine and determination, and the fruits of his labor were finally taking shape on the screen. The new automation script he'd been developing was nearing completion, its intricate algorithms designed to streamline a critical process and save the team countless hours of manual work.

Ethan leaned back in his chair, exhaustion tugging at his eyelids, but a grin spreading across his face. He'd faced a formidable challenge, wrestled with complex logic, and emerged victorious. The script was elegant, efficient, and, most importantly, it worked.

He ran a final test, his heart pounding with anticipation. The script executed flawlessly, the results displayed on the screen in a satisfying cascade of green text. Ethan let out a whoop of triumph, the sound echoing through the mostly deserted office. He'd done it. He'd conquered the code, tamed the data, and emerged as a champion of automation.

The next morning, he presented his work to the team, his voice trembling slightly with a mix of nerves and excitement. Megan, ever the pragmatist, peppered him with questions, her sharp mind dissecting the logic, probing for weaknesses. But the script held up under scrutiny, its efficiency and accuracy undeniable.

Even Noah, the stoic overlord of Operations, offered a rare nod of approval. "Good work, Ethan," he said, his voice devoid of inflection, yet somehow conveying a sense of acknowledgement that Ethan hadn't expected. "This will save us valuable time and resources."

Ethan's chest swelled with pride. He'd done it. He'd impressed Noah, the man whose approval he craved more than anyone else's. He'd proven himself, not just as a competent employee, but as a valuable asset to the team.

But as the day wore on, a strange feeling crept into Ethan's mind, a subtle unease that gnawed at the edges of his triumph. He'd achieved a significant victory, earned the recognition he'd been striving for, yet a nagging voice whispered doubts in his ear.

Was this it? he wondered, staring out the window at the bustling cityscape, the endless stream of cars and people a blur of motion. Was this the pinnacle of his career, a script that automated a process? Was this what he'd dreamed of when he'd envisioned his future?

He thought about his friends, the ones who were pursuing their passions, building their own businesses, creating something new and exciting. He thought about his girlfriend, Lauren, her artistic spirit, her unwavering belief in the power of creativity and self-expression. And he thought about himself, stuck in a cubicle, staring at spreadsheets and code, his days a blur of meetings, deadlines, and performance reviews.

A wave of self-doubt washed over him, threatening to drown his newfound confidence.

Was he on the right path? he wondered. Was he fulfilling his potential? Was he even happy?

The questions swirled in his mind, a vortex of uncertainty that pulled him deeper into a spiral of doubt. He felt lost, adrift in a sea of possibilities, his compass spinning wildly, unable to find true north.

He sought solace in the familiar comfort of the break room, the aroma of freshly brewed coffee a temporary distraction from his inner turmoil. Mila found him there, her ever-present tumbler in hand, her eyes sparkling with a mix of amusement and concern.

"You look like you've just seen a ghost," she quipped, her voice a welcome intrusion into his brooding silence.

Ethan managed a weak smile. "Worse. I think I've just seen my future, and it's filled with spreadsheets and code."

Mila's expression softened. "What's going on, Ethan?"

Ethan hesitated, unsure how to articulate the jumble of thoughts and emotions swirling within him. "I don't know," he finally admitted, his voice barely a whisper. "I just... I feel lost. I thought I was on the right track, but now I'm not so sure."

Mila nodded, her gaze steady and reassuring. "It's okay to feel lost, Ethan. It's part of the journey. We all go through it at some point, especially when we're starting out. It's like being in a maze – you might think you're heading towards the exit, but then you hit a dead end, and you have to find a new path."

She paused, her eyes searching his. "But the important thing is to keep moving, to keep exploring, to keep searching for the path that feels right for you. And don't be afraid to ask for help along the way. We're all here to support you, to guide you, to help you find your way."

Ethan's shoulders relaxed slightly, the tension easing. Mila's words were like a lifeline, a beacon of hope in the midst of his uncertainty.

"Thanks, Mila," he said, his voice thick with gratitude. "I needed to hear that."

"Anytime," she said, her smile warm and genuine. "Now, tell me – what is it that you really want? What's your vision for the future?"

Ethan's mind raced, the question echoing through the chambers of his heart. What did he want? What was his vision? He'd never really thought about it before, not in those terms. He'd always focused on the next task, the next deadline, the next promotion. But what about the bigger picture? What about the life he wanted to create, the impact he wanted to make, the legacy he wanted to leave behind?

He thought about his passions, his interests, the things that made his heart sing. He thought about the problems he wanted to solve, the challenges he wanted to overcome, the world he wanted to create. And slowly, a vision began to emerge, a hazy image that gradually sharpened into focus.

He saw himself as a leader, not just in the workplace, but in the world. He saw himself using his skills and talents to make a difference, to inspire others, to create something meaningful and lasting. He saw himself as a bridge between generations, a catalyst for change, a champion for innovation and collaboration.

The vision was still blurry, the details yet to be defined, but it was there, a spark of inspiration that ignited a fire within him. He felt a surge of excitement, a renewed sense of purpose, a determination to break through his barriers and pursue his dreams.

He looked at Mila, his eyes shining with newfound clarity. "I want to make a difference," he said, his voice firm and resolute. "I want to use my skills to create something better, to leave the world a little bit better than I found it."

Mila smiled, her eyes twinkling with approval. "That's a great vision, Ethan. And I have no doubt that you can achieve it. Just remember – the journey won't be easy. There will be challenges, setbacks, and moments of doubt. But as long as you hold onto your vision, as long as you keep moving forward, you'll get there."

Ethan nodded, his heart filled with gratitude and determination. He had a vision now, a guiding star to lead him through the darkness, a beacon of hope to illuminate his path. And he knew, with a certainty that transcended his doubts and fears, that he was ready for the journey.

As he left the break room, a new energy coursed through him, a sense of purpose that propelled him forward. He returned to his desk, his fingers flying across the keyboard, his mind buzzing with ideas. He was no longer just an employee, a cog in the corporate machine; he was a visionary, a leader, a force for change.

And he was ready to take on the world.

CHAPTER XVII

# Trial by Fire

The fluorescent lights of the office hummed overhead, casting a sterile glow on the tense faces gathered around the conference table. Ethan fidgeted in his chair, the worn leather offering little comfort against the knot of anxiety tightening in his stomach. Across the table, Noah's expression was a mask of controlled concern, his brow furrowed, his lips pressed into a thin line. The air crackled with a tension thicker than the stale coffee that fueled their late-night work sessions.

"The client's threatening to pull the account," Megan announced, her voice steady, but her eyes betraying the gravity of the situation. "They're claiming a critical error in our data analysis has cost them significant revenue."

A collective gasp rippled through the room, the sound punctuated by the frantic tapping of fingers on keyboards as the team scrambled to access the relevant data, their faces illuminated by the eerie glow of their monitors. Ethan's heart hammered against his ribs, a frantic drumbeat echoing the rising panic in his chest. He could feel the blood draining from his face, his carefully constructed composure crumbling like a poorly built sandcastle.

"What kind of error?" Noah's voice cut through the chaos, sharp and demanding, his gaze sweeping across the room like a hawk searching for prey. "Who was responsible for this analysis?"

Ethan's breath hitched. He knew the answer before Megan even spoke. It was his analysis. His responsibility. His mistake.

"It was Ethan's analysis," Megan confirmed, her voice laced with a mixture of sympathy and disappointment. "He was tasked with validating the data for the Peterson account last week."

Ethan's gaze dropped to the table, his cheeks burning with shame. He could feel the weight of a dozen pairs of eyes on him, their judgment a tangible force that threatened to crush him. He wanted to disappear, to melt into the chair and become one with the conference room furniture, to escape the suffocating scrutiny of his colleagues.

"Ethan," Noah's voice was like ice shards, piercing through Ethan's self-recrimination, "explain yourself."

Ethan's voice caught in his throat, the words refusing to form. He opened his mouth, but all that emerged was a strangled gasp, a pathetic sound that amplified his humiliation. He could feel the tears pricking at his eyes, a wave of self-pity threatening to overwhelm him.

"I... I don't know what happened," he finally stammered, his voice barely a whisper. "I checked the data, I ran the validations, I followed the protocols. I don't understand how this could have happened."

"That's not good enough, Ethan," Noah's voice was sharper now, laced with a chilling disappointment. "This isn't a game. This is our client's business, their livelihood. Your mistake has cost them money, and it's put our entire company at risk."

Ethan's vision blurred, the tears finally spilling over, hot and stinging against his cheeks. He felt like a child being scolded, his carefully constructed image of competence and confidence shattered into a million pieces.

"I'm sorry," he choked out, his voice thick with emotion. "I didn't mean to... I didn't..."

He couldn't finish the sentence. The shame was overwhelming, suffocating, a crushing weight that threatened to drown him.

Noah's expression softened slightly, a flicker of empathy crossing his usually stoic features. He'd been there himself, years ago, the weight of responsibility pressing down on him, the fear of failure a constant companion. He recognized the panic in Ethan's eyes, the desperation in his voice.

"Ethan," he said, his tone gentler now, "I know you didn't intend for this to happen. But that doesn't change the fact that it did. We need to fix this, and we need to do it now."

He stood up, his chair scraping against the floor, the sound a jarring interruption to the tense silence that had settled over the room. "Everyone, back to your desks," he commanded, his voice regaining its usual authority. "We're in crisis mode. Ethan, you stay here."

The room emptied quickly, the team members scattering like frightened birds, leaving Ethan alone with Noah, the silence between them heavier than ever.

Noah walked around the table, his footsteps echoing in the suddenly empty space. He stopped in front of Ethan, his gaze intense, searching.

"Ethan," he said, his voice low and steady, "I need you to pull yourself together. We don't have time for tears. We need solutions."

Ethan took a deep breath, wiping his eyes with the back of his hand, the gesture a pathetic attempt to regain some semblance of composure. "What do we do?" he asked, his voice trembling.

"We find the error," Noah said, his tone firm, resolute. "We fix it. And we make it right with the client."

He placed a hand on Ethan's shoulder, the touch surprisingly gentle, a gesture of support that Ethan hadn't expected. "I know you're scared," he said, his voice softening further. "But you're not alone in this. We're a team, and we'll get through this together."

Ethan looked up, his eyes meeting Noah's, a flicker of gratitude and determination sparking within him. He wasn't alone. He had Noah, he had Mila, he had the team. And together, they would find a way to fix this.

The weight on his shoulders didn't disappear entirely, but it lessened, replaced by a newfound resolve. He would face this challenge head-on, learn from his mistakes, and emerge stronger, more resilient, more capable.

He would prove to Noah, to the team, and to himself that he was worthy of their trust, that he could be counted on, that he was more than just a rookie who made mistakes. He was Ethan, and he was ready to fight.

CHAPTER XVIII

# Forging a Partnership in the Crucible of Crisis

The silence in the conference room was thick with tension, heavy and suffocating, pressing down on Ethan like a physical weight. He could feel the blood draining from his face, his skin clammy, his heart pounding a frantic rhythm against his ribs. Across the table, Noah's expression was a mask of controlled concern, his brow furrowed, his lips pressed into a thin line, his eyes sharp and piercing, like a hawk assessing its prey. The air crackled with a tension thicker than the stale coffee that fueled their late-night work sessions, a tension that spoke of deadlines missed, expectations unmet, and trust betrayed.

"The client's threatening to pull the account," Megan announced, her voice steady, a calm amidst the storm, but her eyes betraying the gravity of the situation, the potential fallout that could ripple through the entire company. "They're claiming a critical error in our data analysis has cost them significant revenue."

A collective gasp rippled through the room, a wave of shock and disbelief washing over the team. The sound was punctuated by the frantic tapping of fingers on keyboards as the team members scrambled to access the relevant data, their faces illuminated by the eerie glow of their monitors, their eyes wide with a mixture of fear and confusion. Ethan's heart hammered against his ribs, a frantic drumbeat echoing the rising panic in his chest. He could feel his carefully constructed composure crumbling like a poorly built sandcastle, the grains of his confidence slipping away with each passing second.

"What kind of error?" Noah's voice cut through the chaos, sharp and demanding, his gaze sweeping across the room like a hawk searching for prey. "Who was responsible for this analysis?"

Ethan's breath hitched. He knew the answer before Megan even spoke. It was his analysis. His responsibility. His mistake. The realization hit him like a punch to the gut, the air knocked out of his lungs, his carefully constructed world tilting on its axis.

"It was Ethan's analysis," Megan confirmed, her voice laced with a mixture of sympathy and disappointment, her eyes conveying a message of understanding and regret. "He was tasked with validating the data for the

Peterson account last week."

Ethan's gaze dropped to the table, his cheeks burning with shame, the intricate wood grain suddenly the most fascinating thing in the world. He could feel the weight of a dozen pairs of eyes on him, their judgment a tangible force that threatened to crush him. He wanted to disappear, to melt into the chair and become one with the conference room furniture, to escape the suffocating scrutiny of his colleagues, the disappointment in Noah's eyes, the pity in Megan's.

"Ethan," Noah's voice was like ice shards, piercing through Ethan's self-recrimination, shattering the fragile shell of his composure. "Explain yourself."

Ethan's voice caught in his throat, the words refusing to form, trapped behind a wall of shame and fear. He opened his mouth, but all that emerged was a strangled gasp, a pathetic sound that amplified his humiliation, his sense of inadequacy. He could feel the tears pricking at his eyes, hot and unwelcome, a wave of self-pity threatening to overwhelm him.

"I... I don't know what happened," he finally stammered, his voice barely a whisper, a pathetic plea for understanding. "I checked the data, I ran the validations, I followed the protocols. I don't understand how this could have happened. I... I..."

He couldn't finish the sentence. The words wouldn't come. The shame was too overwhelming, suffocating him, crushing him beneath its weight. He felt like a child again, caught in a lie, exposed and vulnerable, his carefully constructed image of competence and confidence shattered into a million pieces.

Noah's expression softened slightly, a flicker of empathy crossing his usually stoic features. He'd been there himself, years ago, the weight of responsibility pressing down on him, the fear of failure a constant companion. He recognized the panic in Ethan's eyes, the desperation in his voice, the raw vulnerability that lay beneath the surface of his carefully constructed persona.

"Ethan," he said, his tone gentler now, a hint of understanding in his voice, "I know you didn't intend for this to happen. But that doesn't change the fact that it did. We need to fix this, and we need to do it now."

He stood up, his chair scraping against the floor, the sound a jarring interruption to the tense silence that had settled over the room. "Everyone, back to your desks," he commanded, his voice regaining its usual authority, the steel returning to his spine. "We're in crisis mode. Ethan, you stay here."

The room emptied quickly, the team members scattering like frightened birds, their footsteps echoing in the suddenly silent space. They left behind a trail of unfinished coffee cups, crumpled notes, and a lingering sense of anxiety that clung to the air like a shroud. Ethan and Noah were left alone, the silence between them heavier than ever, the weight of the situation pressing down on them like a physical force.

Noah walked around the table, his footsteps measured and deliberate, each step a declaration of purpose, of control. He stopped in front of Ethan, his gaze intense, searching, piercing through the younger man's facade, seeking the truth, the vulnerability, the spark of resilience that lay beneath the surface.

"Ethan," he said, his voice low and steady, a calming presence in the midst of the storm, "I need you to pull yourself together. We don't have time for tears. We need solutions. We need action. We need you."

Ethan took a deep breath, wiping his eyes with the back of his hand, the gesture a pathetic attempt to regain some semblance of composure, to reclaim the image of competence he'd worked so hard to cultivate. "What do we do?" he asked, his voice trembling, but the hint of a challenge, a spark of defiance, flickering in his eyes.

"We find the error," Noah said, his tone firm, resolute, a beacon of determination in the sea of uncertainty. "We fix it. And we make it right with the client. We don't give up. We don't back down. We fight."

He pulled up a chair beside Ethan, their knees almost touching, the proximity a silent acknowledgment of their shared struggle, their shared responsibility. It was a gesture of solidarity, a message of support that transcended the usual boundaries of their professional relationship.

"I need you to walk me through your analysis," he said, his voice softer now, the sharp edge of his earlier reprimand replaced by a tone of collaboration, of partnership. "Tell me exactly what you did, step by step. Don't leave anything out. Show me your process, your thinking, your doubts. Let me see the world through your eyes."

Ethan hesitated for a moment, his fingers tracing the worn edges of his notebook, his mind a whirlwind of self-recrimination and doubt. But then he took a deep breath, his shoulders squaring slightly, and began to speak, his voice gaining strength with each word, the fear and shame receding as he immersed himself in the task at hand.

He described the data he'd used, the validation protocols he'd followed, the assumptions he'd made. He laid bare his process, his vulnerabilities, his uncertainties, his thought processes, his doubts, his fears. He didn't hold back, didn't try to sugarcoat or justify. He was honest, raw, vulnerable. And as he spoke, Noah listened intently, his mind racing, searching for patterns, for anomalies, for any clue that could lead them to the source of the error.

Hours passed, the clock ticking relentlessly, the silence punctuated only by the rhythmic tapping of keyboards and the occasional frustrated sigh. They worked side by side, their initial tension gradually easing into a focused collaboration, a shared determination to find the solution, to salvage the situation, to protect the company and its clients. They were no longer just boss and employee, but partners in a shared struggle, their individual strengths complementing each other, their combined efforts creating a synergy that was greater than the sum of their parts.

Ethan, fueled by a mix of adrenaline and remorse, dove deep into the data, his fingers flying across the keyboard, his eyes scanning the endless rows and columns, searching for the elusive error that had triggered this crisis. He was relentless, his focus unwavering, his determination fueled by a desire to redeem himself, to prove his worth, to show Noah and the team that he could be trusted, that he could rise to the occasion.

Noah, with his methodical approach and years of experience, provided a steady hand, guiding Ethan's analysis, questioning his assumptions, and offering alternative perspectives. He was the anchor, the voice of reason, the one who kept Ethan grounded, preventing him from spiraling into despair, reminding him that every challenge, every setback, was an opportunity for growth, for learning, for becoming a better version of himself.

The breakthrough came late in the evening, a subtle anomaly in the data that had been overlooked in the initial analysis. Ethan, his eyes bleary with exhaustion, his mind numb from hours of staring at spreadsheets, suddenly spotted the discrepancy, a flicker of recognition sparking in his mind, a jolt of adrenaline coursing through his veins.

"There!" he exclaimed, pointing at the screen, his voice hoarse with fatigue but laced with a triumphant edge. "That's it! The decimal point... it's in the wrong place. It's a simple typo, but it throws off the entire calculation. It's like a single misplaced comma in a sentence – it can change the entire meaning."

Noah leaned closer, his eyes scanning the data, his mind racing to confirm Ethan's discovery. And then he saw it, the tiny error that had caused such a monumental crisis, a misplaced decimal point that had skewed the results, misled the client, and threatened to derail the entire project. It was a simple mistake, a careless oversight, but in the world of data analysis, even the smallest error could have catastrophic consequences.

A wave of relief washed over him, followed by a surge of admiration for Ethan's persistence, his determination to find the solution, his refusal to give up even in the face of overwhelming pressure. He had doubted Ethan, had questioned his abilities, his maturity, his readiness for the challenges of the corporate world. But Ethan had proven him wrong, had risen to the occasion, had demonstrated a resilience and a dedication that Noah hadn't expected.

"You found it," he said, his voice filled with a mixture of gratitude and pride, his expression softening, the lines around his eyes crinkling with a genuine smile that Ethan had rarely seen before. "You saved the day, Ethan. You saved the account. You saved us."

Ethan's face flushed with a mix of embarrassment and relief, the tears that had threatened to overwhelm him earlier now receding, replaced by a quiet sense of accomplishment. "It was my mistake in the first place," he mumbled, his voice still laced with shame, but the self-recrimination tempered by the knowledge that he had redeemed himself, that he had proven his worth.

"We all make mistakes, Ethan," Noah said, his tone gentle but firm, his hand still resting on Ethan's shoulder, a reassuring presence in the midst of the lingering tension. "The important thing is that you found it, you fixed it, and you learned from it. That's what matters. That's what defines us."

He stood up, stretching his stiff muscles, his gaze meeting Ethan's, a silent acknowledgment of the bond that had formed between them, the partnership forged in the crucible of crisis. "Now, go home and get some rest. You've earned it."

Ethan nodded, his exhaustion finally catching up with him, the adrenaline that had fueled him through the long hours fading, leaving behind a bone-deep weariness. He gathered his things, his footsteps heavy as he walked towards the door, the weight of the day pressing down on him, but also a lightness in his heart, a sense of accomplishment that he hadn't felt before.

As he reached the threshold, he paused, turning back to look at Noah, his eyes filled with a mixture of gratitude and respect.

"Thank you," he said, his voice sincere, filled with a newfound understanding of the man who had once seemed so distant, so intimidating.

"For everything."

Noah nodded, a faint smile still playing on his lips. "You're welcome, Ethan. And don't worry, we'll get through this. Together."

Ethan left the office, the city lights a blur through his tired eyes, the sounds of the city a distant hum against the backdrop of his own thoughts. He was exhausted, emotionally drained, but there was a lightness in his step, a sense of accomplishment that he hadn't felt before. He'd made a mistake, a costly one, but he'd also risen to the challenge, faced his fears, and proven himself capable of handling the pressure. And he'd done it with Noah by his side, not as a critic or a judge, but as a mentor, a partner, a fellow traveler on the unpredictable journey of life.

CHAPTER XIX

# Bridges Built in the Ashes of Breakdown

The silence in Noah's office was a stark contrast to the chaos that had consumed the team just hours earlier. The air, usually thick with the hum of productivity and the clatter of keyboards, was still, heavy with the lingering scent of stale coffee and nervous energy. Ethan sat perched on the edge of the chair opposite Noah's desk, his fingers tracing the worn edges of his notebook, his gaze fixed on the intricate patterns of the Persian rug beneath his feet, each swirl and flourish a testament to the meticulous craftsmanship that had gone into its creation.

Noah, his usually stoic features softened by a weariness that Ethan had never witnessed before, leaned back in his chair, the worn leather creaking softly beneath his weight. His gaze drifted towards the window, drawn to the mesmerizing tapestry of the cityscape beyond. The city lights twinkled like a constellation of dreams and aspirations, a vibrant symphony of ambition and resilience, a stark contrast to the quiet introspection that filled the room.

"Ethan," Noah began, his voice rough with exhaustion, the usual crispness replaced by a vulnerability that surprised Ethan, "I owe you an apology."

Ethan's head snapped up, his eyes widening in disbelief. An apology? From Noah? The man who seemed to embody unwavering strength and control, the one who rarely admitted to any weakness, let alone a mistake? It was as if the earth had shifted beneath his feet, the familiar landscape of their relationship suddenly tilting on its axis.

"I pushed you too hard," Noah continued, his gaze meeting Ethan's, the sincerity in his eyes undeniable, a depth of emotion that Ethan had never seen before. "I held you to a standard that you weren't ready for, that you didn't even understand. I expected you to be perfect, to be infallible, to be... me."

He paused, his gaze dropping to his hands, the lines and calluses a testament to the years of hard work, the battles fought and won, the scars that remained as a permanent reminder of the journey he had taken. "I saw in you a reflection of my younger self," he confessed, his voice barely a whisper, the words heavy with regret and a newfound understanding. "The ambition, the drive, the impatience. But I forgot that you're not me. You're Ethan. And you have your own path to forge, your own lessons to learn, your own mistakes to make."

Ethan's heart ached for Noah, the man who had always seemed so invincible, so unyielding, now revealing a vulnerability that resonated deep within him. He saw in Noah's confession a reflection of his own struggles, his own fears, his own desperate need for acceptance and validation. He saw a kindred spirit, a fellow traveler on the unpredictable journey of life, a mentor who was also a human being, flawed and vulnerable, yet still striving for excellence.

"Noah," he began, his voice hesitant, unsure how to navigate this unfamiliar territory of emotional honesty, "I... I also owe you an apology. I was reckless, impulsive. I didn't fully understand the consequences of my actions, the impact they could have on the team, on the company, on our clients. I was so focused on proving myself, on earning your approval, that I forgot about the bigger picture."

He paused, his gaze dropping to his own hands, the smooth skin a stark contrast to Noah's weathered ones, a visual reminder of the journey that lay ahead of him, the lessons he had yet to learn, the experiences that would shape him, mold him, and ultimately define him.

"I'm still learning," he admitted, his voice gaining strength, his resolve solidifying. "But I'm learning fast. And I'm grateful for your guidance, even when it's tough, even when it hurts. Because I know you're pushing me to be better, to be stronger, to be the best version of myself."

A comfortable silence settled between them, a shared understanding that transcended words. The air crackled with a newfound connection, a bridge built between two generations, two perspectives, two individuals who had once seemed worlds apart, but now found themselves standing on common ground, united by their shared experiences, their shared vulnerabilities, their shared humanity.

"I'm not perfect, Ethan," Noah said finally, his voice regaining its strength, but the edges softened, the harshness replaced by a quiet sincerity. "I make mistakes. I have doubts. I struggle. But I've learned that it's okay to not be okay. It's okay to ask for help. It's okay to lean on others. And it's okay to let others lean on you."

He looked at Ethan, his eyes filled with a warmth that Ethan had rarely seen before, a warmth that melted the icy facade he usually wore, revealing the compassionate heart that beat beneath. "We're a team, Ethan. And that means we support each other, we challenge each other, and we grow together. We don't give up on each other. We don't let each other down. We rise together."

Ethan's heart swelled with gratitude and a newfound respect for the man who had once seemed so intimidating, so unapproachable. He saw in Noah not just a boss, but a mentor, a guide, a fellow traveler on the unpredictable journey of life, someone who understood the struggles, the doubts, the fears that came with the territory of being human.

"Thank you, Noah," he said, his voice filled with emotion, the words inadequate to express the depth of his gratitude, the profound shift in their relationship.

Noah nodded, a genuine smile gracing his lips, a rare and precious sight that illuminated the room, chasing away the shadows of doubt and fear. "You're welcome, Ethan. And don't worry, we'll get through this. Together."

They sat in silence for a moment, the weight of the past few days lifting, replaced by a sense of hope, a belief in the power of connection, the strength of collaboration. The air thrummed with a newfound energy, a sense of possibility, a shared vision for the future.

"So," Noah said finally, breaking the silence with a chuckle, "what do you say we get out of here and grab a beer? My treat."

Ethan grinned, the tension finally leaving his shoulders, his heart lighter than it had been in weeks. "Sounds good to me, Noah. But you're buying dinner too. I'm starving."

As they left the office, the city lights seemed to twinkle a little brighter, the sounds of the city a symphony of possibilities, a vibrant backdrop to their newfound camaraderie. They walked side by side, their footsteps echoing in the quiet streets, their conversation flowing easily, the boundaries between boss and employee blurring, replaced by a camaraderie that transcended their professional roles.

They talked about their families, their dreams, their fears, their hopes for the future. They shared stories, laughter, and a newfound understanding of each other, their voices mingling with the city's hum, creating a harmonious melody of connection and shared experience. And as they walked, they realized that the crisis they had faced together had not just brought them closer, it had forged a bond, a partnership that would shape not just their professional lives, but their personal journeys as well.

They were no longer just colleagues, they were friends. And they knew, with a certainty that transcended words, that they would face whatever challenges lay ahead, together.

CHAPTER XX

# A New Face, a Familiar Frustration

The Monday morning sun sliced through the blinds, casting sharp lines across Ethan's bedroom floor, a stark contrast to the soft shadows that clung to the corners of the room. He stretched, a groan escaping his lips as he reluctantly peeled himself away from the warmth of his duvet, the soft cotton a comforting cocoon against the chill of the February air. The weekend had been a blessed respite from the relentless grind of the office, a whirlwind of overdue relaxation and reconnection. Long walks with Lauren, their laughter echoing through the crisp winter air, their hands intertwined, a silent testament to the bond that was slowly rebuilding itself after weeks of neglect. A movie marathon with friends, the glow of the screen illuminating their faces, their shared laughter a comforting balm against the anxieties that gnawed at the edges of their carefree camaraderie. And a blessedly empty inbox, a digital sanctuary from the endless stream of emails, deadlines, and demands that usually cluttered his screen.

But the respite was over. The alarm clock's insistent chirping shattered the remnants of his peaceful slumber, a harsh reminder that the real world awaited, with its spreadsheets, its deadlines, and its ever-present pressure to perform. The familiar knot of anticipation – and a hint of dread – tightened in his stomach as he thought about returning to the office, to the demanding gaze of Noah, the unpredictable whims of the clients, and the ever-shifting landscape of the corporate world.

He showered, the hot water a soothing balm against the lingering chill of the night, the steam swirling and rising like his own conflicted thoughts. What if this new employee is a total nightmare? What if I can't handle the pressure? What if I screw up again and lose Noah's trust? The questions chased each other around his mind, a relentless chorus of self-doubt that threatened to drown out the quiet confidence he'd been building over the past few weeks.

He dressed, the familiar routine of selecting a shirt, pants, and shoes a grounding ritual, a preparation for the day ahead. He forced himself to choose a crisp button-down and a pair of well-worn chinos, a compromise between his desire for comfort and the need to project an image of professionalism, of competence, of someone who had it all together. He grabbed a bagel from the bakery downstairs, the warm, yeasty scent a comforting reminder of simpler times, of childhood mornings spent with his family, the aroma of freshly baked bread filling the kitchen, a promise of warmth and nourishment.

As he stepped into the SynergyWorks office, the usual buzz of activity enveloped him – the clatter of keyboards, a symphony of productivity; the murmur of conversations, a tapestry of ideas and anxieties; the faint scent of stale coffee and ambition, a potent cocktail that fueled the relentless pursuit of success. But there was a new element this morning, a discordant note in the usual symphony of productivity, a subtle shift in the atmosphere that made Ethan's senses tingle with a mix of curiosity and apprehension.

He spotted Noah by the coffee machine, his usual stern expression softened by a faint smile, a rare sight that made Ethan pause, his eyebrows furrowing in surprise. Noah was chatting with a young woman Ethan had never seen before, her back to him, her posture a study in casual indifference. She was slouched against the counter, her eyes half-closed, a bored expression on her face as she scrolled through her phone, her fingers dancing across the screen with a practiced ease that spoke of countless hours spent in the digital realm. Her attire was a study in casual Friday, even though it was Monday: ripped jeans, a faded band t-shirt that proclaimed her allegiance to a rock band Ethan had never heard of, and a pair of sneakers that looked like they'd been through a war zone, their once-bright colors faded and scuffed, the laces frayed and untied.

Ethan felt a surge of irritation, a wave of disapproval that he quickly suppressed. He'd been in her shoes not so long ago, the casual disregard for appearances, the nonchalant attitude, the sense of entitlement that came with being young and inexperienced. He'd learned the hard way that in the corporate world, appearances mattered, that professionalism and attention to detail were not just empty formalities, but essential tools for building trust and credibility.

"Ethan," Noah called out, his voice carrying a hint of forced enthusiasm that surprised Ethan, "come meet our newest team member, Riley."

Ethan approached, a polite smile plastered on his face, his mind buzzing with questions. Who was this Riley? What was her role? And why did she seem to exude an air of nonchalant indifference that grated on his nerves, a stark contrast to the eager enthusiasm he'd displayed just a few months ago? He couldn't help but wonder if this was what Noah saw in him when he first started, a raw, unpolished potential that needed to be molded and refined.

"Riley, this is Ethan," Noah continued, gesturing towards Ethan with a forced enthusiasm that made Ethan cringe. He could sense the desperation in Noah's voice, the thinly veiled plea for Ethan to welcome this new addition to the team, to embrace the change, to adapt to the ever-shifting dynamics of the workplace. "He's one of our rising stars in Operations, a creative mind with a knack for problem-solving. He's been instrumental in streamlining our workflows and improving our efficiency."

Riley barely looked up from her phone, her fingers still dancing across the screen, her attention seemingly consumed by the digital world that unfolded before her. "Sup," she mumbled, her voice flat, devoid of any discernible interest or enthusiasm.

Ethan's eyebrows shot up, his surprise quickly morphing into a wave of disapproval. Was this how the new generation greeted their colleagues? No handshake? No eye contact? No semblance of professional courtesy? He felt a surge of irritation, a wave of disapproval that he quickly suppressed. He had to remind himself that he was the senior employee now, the one responsible for setting a good example, for guiding and mentoring those who were new to the corporate world.

"Nice to meet you, Riley," he said, extending his hand, his voice a touch too formal, a subtle rebuke to her casual disregard for the unspoken rules of professional etiquette. He hoped that his formality would serve as a gentle nudge, a subtle reminder that the workplace had its own set of expectations, its own code of conduct.

Riley finally looked up, her eyes meeting his with a flicker of annoyance, as if he were interrupting something far more important than a simple introduction. She reluctantly extended her hand, her grip limp and lifeless, a stark contrast to the firm handshake that Ethan had come to expect from his colleagues. "Yeah, whatever," she mumbled, her gaze returning to her phone, her disinterest palpable.

Ethan's jaw tightened. He could feel his patience wearing thin, the carefully constructed composure he'd been cultivating over the past few months threatening to crack under the weight of Riley's blatant disregard for the norms of the workplace. This Riley was everything he'd been trying to overcome – the entitlement, the lack of effort, the disregard for the rules and expectations that held the team together. He glanced at Noah, hoping for some intervention, some guidance on how to handle this unexpected challenge, this unwelcome disruption to the carefully balanced ecosystem of the Operations team.

But Noah just smiled, a strained smile that didn't reach his eyes, a smile that spoke of resignation and a hint of desperation. "Riley's going to be working closely with you on the upcoming data migration project," he explained, his voice laced with a forced optimism that Ethan found unsettling. "She's got a... unique perspective on data analysis. I'm confident that you two will... learn a lot from each other."

Ethan's stomach churned, a wave of nausea rising in his throat. Learn a lot from each other? What was that supposed to mean? Was he expected to mentor this entitled slacker? To teach her the basics of professionalism and work ethic? To mold her into a productive member of the team, while simultaneously juggling his own responsibilities and navigating the ever-increasing demands of his job? He felt a surge of resentment, a wave of frustration that threatened to spill over, to shatter the carefully constructed image of calm competence he'd been working so hard to maintain.

He took a deep breath, reminding himself of the lessons he'd learned, the progress he'd made. He wouldn't let Riley's negativity drag him down. He wouldn't let her entitlement and apathy poison the atmosphere of the team. He would rise above it, be the leader he was meant to be, and guide her towards a more productive and fulfilling path.

"Okay, Riley," he said, his voice firm but patient, a careful balance of authority and encouragement. "Let's get started. We've got a lot of work to do, and I want to make sure we're both on the same page. We need to understand the scope of the project, the deadlines, the expectations, the potential challenges. We need to establish a clear plan, a roadmap to success, a strategy that will allow us to leverage our individual strengths and achieve our shared goals."

He launched into a detailed explanation of the project, outlining the key objectives, the timelines, the deliverables, and the potential roadblocks. He described the data migration process, the validation protocols, the quality assurance checks, and the communication channels they would be using. He spoke with passion and clarity, his enthusiasm tempered by a newfound understanding of the importance of precision and attention to detail.

Riley, however, seemed unimpressed. She stifled a yawn, her eyes glazing over as Ethan spoke, her fingers still tapping away at her phone, her attention clearly elsewhere. Ethan could feel his frustration mounting, his patience wearing thin.

"Riley," he said, his voice sharper now, a hint of warning creeping into his tone, "are you even listening to me?"

Riley looked up, her eyes narrowed, a flicker of defiance in their depths. "Yeah, yeah, whatever," she mumbled, rolling her eyes. "It's just a data migration project. How hard can it be?"

Ethan's jaw clenched, his patience snapping like a dry twig. This was not how he had envisioned their first interaction, their first step towards a collaborative partnership. He had hoped for enthusiasm, for engagement, for a willingness to learn and contribute. Instead, he was met with apathy, disinterest, and a blatant disregard for the importance of the task at hand.

He took a deep breath, reminding himself of Noah's words, of the lessons he had learned about patience, understanding, and the importance of meeting people where they were. He wouldn't let Riley's negativity derail the project, nor would he let her undermine his own commitment to excellence.

"Riley," he said, his voice calm but firm, "this project is not 'just a data migration.' It's a critical component of our company's growth strategy. It's an opportunity for us to improve our efficiency, enhance our data security, and provide better service to our clients. It's a challenge that demands our full attention, our dedication, and our commitment to excellence."

He paused, his gaze meeting hers, a silent challenge in his eyes. "I know you're new to the team, and I understand that you might not fully grasp the significance of this project yet. But I assure you, it's important. And I expect you to treat it as such."

Riley's expression shifted, the boredom replaced by a flicker of curiosity, a hint of respect. Ethan's words had struck a chord, had pierced through her facade of indifference, had awakened a spark of interest that he hadn't expected.

"Okay, fine," she said, her voice softer now, a hint of grudging respect in her tone. "I get it. It's important. So what do you want me to do?"

Ethan smiled, a genuine smile that reached his eyes, a smile that spoke of hope and encouragement. He had broken through, had connected with Riley on a level that transcended her initial apathy. He had sparked her interest, had ignited a flicker of motivation, had planted the seeds of a potential partnership.

"I'm glad you asked," he said, his voice filled with a newfound enthusiasm. "Let's start by reviewing the project plan together. I want to make sure you understand the scope of the work, the timelines, the deliverables, and the potential challenges. Then we can discuss your specific role, your strengths, and how you can best contribute to the team's success."

Riley nodded, her gaze fixed on Ethan, her expression a mixture of curiosity and apprehension. She was still unsure, still hesitant, but there was a spark of interest in her eyes, a glimmer of potential that Ethan was determined to nurture.

He pulled out the project plan, spreading it across the table, his fingers tracing the lines, the charts, the diagrams that represented the complex web of tasks and dependencies that lay ahead. He explained the process, the challenges, the opportunities, his voice filled with passion and clarity, his enthusiasm contagious.

And as he spoke, he watched as Riley's expression shifted, the boredom fading, replaced by a growing focus, a dawning understanding, a spark of engagement that warmed Ethan's heart. He had found a way to connect with her, to ignite her interest, to awaken her potential.

He had a feeling that this project, this unexpected partnership, was going to be more than just a data migration. It was going to be a journey of discovery, a learning experience, a chance for both of them to grow, to evolve, to become better versions of themselves. And he was excited to see where it would lead them.

CHAPTER XXI

# Same Generation, but?

The frustration simmered within Ethan, a low burn that threatened to erupt with every eye roll, every dismissive shrug, every "like, whatever" that punctuated Riley's vocabulary. He'd tried to be patient, to be understanding, to channel the wisdom he'd gleaned from Noah and Mila about mentorship and leadership. But Riley's nonchalance was a constant test, a challenge to his every carefully cultivated instinct.

It wasn't just her lackadaisical attitude that grated on him; it was the subtle air of entitlement that clung to her like an expensive perfume, the unspoken assumption that the world owed her something, that she was destined for greatness simply by virtue of her existence. He'd seen it before, in college, in those students who coasted through on their parents' wealth and connections, who never had to face the struggle, the grind, the sheer determination that it took to forge your own path.

He'd tried to ignore it, to focus on the task at hand, the data migration project that Noah had entrusted to them. But Riley's apathy was like a virus, infecting the team's morale, slowing their progress, threatening to derail the entire operation. He found himself snapping at her, his voice sharper than intended, his patience wearing thin.

"Riley, this isn't a social media feed," he'd say, his voice tight with frustration, his eyes burning with a mixture of anger and disappointment. "We need to focus, to engage, to contribute. We have deadlines, deliverables, and a team depending on us."

Riley would just sigh dramatically, her eyes glazing over, her fingers resuming their relentless dance across her phone screen, the glow of the display illuminating her face, highlighting the bored expression that seemed permanently etched there. "Okay, boomer," she'd mumble, the dismissive label a stinging reminder of the generational divide that seemed to separate them, despite their shared age. It was a label that Ethan resented, a stereotype that he refused to embody.

He'd tried to reason with her, to explain the importance of the project, the impact it could have on the company, on their clients, on their own careers. But his words seemed to fall on deaf ears, his passion met with a blank stare, his enthusiasm extinguished by her indifference.

"It's just a data migration project," she'd say, her voice flat, devoid of any discernible interest or motivation. "Why are you so stressed about it? It's not like it's going to change the world."

Ethan's frustration reached a boiling point one afternoon, after a particularly unproductive meeting where Riley had contributed nothing but a series of yawns and dismissive shrugs. He'd tried to engage her, to draw her into the discussion, to spark her interest, but his efforts were met with a wall of apathy, a fortress of indifference that he couldn't penetrate.

He stormed into Noah's office, his anger a tangible force that crackled in the air, his footsteps echoing through the quiet hallway, his knuckles white as he gripped the doorknob. He didn't bother knocking, his frustration overriding his usual respect for Noah's authority.

"Noah, we need to talk about Riley," he declared, his voice tight with frustration, his eyes burning with a righteous anger that he couldn't contain. "She's not pulling her weight. She's disengaged, disrespectful, and frankly, a detriment to the team."

Noah leaned back in his chair, his expression unreadable, his eyes studying Ethan with a quiet intensity that made Ethan squirm. He'd seen this before, the frustration of a young employee struggling to navigate the complexities of teamwork, the challenges of managing different personalities and work styles.

"What specifically is the issue, Ethan?" he asked, his voice calm, measured, a stark contrast to Ethan's agitated state.

Ethan paced the room, his words tumbling out in a torrent of frustration, his voice rising and falling with the intensity of his emotions. "She's constantly on her phone, she doesn't contribute to discussions, she misses deadlines, and she treats the whole project like it's a joke. I've tried talking to her, I've tried mentoring her, I've tried everything I can think of, but nothing seems to get through. She's like a brick wall of indifference."

He stopped pacing, his gaze meeting Noah's, his frustration morphing into confusion, a desperate plea for understanding. "I don't understand it," he continued, his voice cracking with a mixture of anger and bewilderment. "We're the same generation, we grew up in the same world, yet she's so... different. So entitled, so apathetic, so... clueless."

Noah nodded slowly, his expression thoughtful, his mind sifting through the layers of Ethan's outburst, searching for the root cause, the underlying issue that was fueling his frustration. He'd seen this before, the clash of personalities, the friction between different work styles, the challenges of building a cohesive team. But there was something more to this, something deeper, something that resonated with his own experiences, his own struggles with generational differences and the complexities of human interaction.

"Ethan," he began, his voice gentle but firm, "have you ever considered that maybe Riley's attitude isn't just a generational thing? Maybe it's something more personal, something rooted in her own experiences, her own upbringing?"

Ethan paused, his mind grappling with this new perspective. He'd been so focused on the generational divide, on the stereotype of the entitled Gen Z, that he hadn't considered the possibility that Riley's behavior might stem from something deeper, something more complex, something that transcended the simplistic labels and generalizations he'd been applying.

"I... I guess not," he admitted, his voice softening, a hint of curiosity replacing the anger. "But what could it be? What could make someone so... disengaged?"

Noah hesitated for a moment, his gaze fixed on a distant point beyond the window, as if searching for the right words, the right way to frame the delicate truth he was about to reveal. He knew that what he was about to say could change Ethan's perception of Riley, could shift the dynamics of the team, could even have repercussions beyond the walls of the office. But he also knew that Ethan deserved to know the truth, that he needed to understand the complexities of the situation, the factors that were shaping Riley's behavior.

"Ethan," he began, his voice low and measured, each word carefully chosen, "Riley is the governor's daughter."

The words hung in the air, heavy with implications, their significance reverberating through Ethan's mind. The governor's daughter? This seemingly apathetic, unmotivated young woman, the one who treated her job like a joke, who couldn't be bothered to contribute to team meetings, who seemed to exist in a perpetual state of boredom and entitlement, was the offspring of one of the most powerful figures in the state?

Suddenly, her behavior made a lot more sense. The sense of entitlement, the lack of urgency, the dismissive attitude towards hard work – it wasn't just a generational thing, it was a product of her upbringing, her environment, the privileged world she had always inhabited.

Ethan's mind reeled, the pieces of the puzzle clicking into place, forming a clearer picture of Riley, her motivations, her challenges, her struggles. He thought about his own upbringing, the values his parents had instilled in him, the importance of curiosity, of agility, of perseverance, of never giving up, of always striving to be better. He thought about the challenges he'd faced, the mistakes he'd made, the lessons he'd learned, the growth he'd experienced.

And he realized that Riley, despite being the same age, from the same generation, had lived a completely different life, a life devoid of the struggles that had shaped him, the challenges that had molded him, the experiences that had defined him. She had never had to worry about paying the rent, about securing a job, about proving her worth. She had never had to taste the bitterness of failure, the sting of rejection, the frustration of setbacks.

"I get it now," Ethan said, his voice filled with a newfound understanding, a touch of empathy for the young woman who had frustrated him so much. "She's never had to learn the lessons that I've learned, the lessons that you've learned. She's never had to face the consequences of her actions, the impact of her choices on others. She's never had to fight for her place in the world."

Noah nodded, his expression softening, a hint of sadness in his eyes. "Exactly. And that's why it's so important for you to be patient with her, to guide her, to mentor her. She needs to learn those lessons, Ethan. She needs to understand the value of hard work, the importance of accountability, the power of collaboration. She needs to see the world through your eyes, through the eyes of someone who has had to fight for every inch of progress, who has had to earn every ounce of respect."

Ethan's shoulders straightened, his resolve solidifying. He wouldn't give up on Riley. He wouldn't let her entitlement and apathy define her. He would be the mentor she needed, the guide who would help her discover the potential within herself, the leader who would show her the way.

"I'll do it, Noah," he said, his voice firm, his gaze steady. "I'll help her. I'll teach her. I'll show her what it means to be a valuable member of this team. I'll show her what it means to be a contributing member of society."

Noah smiled, a genuine smile that reached his eyes, a smile that spoke of trust and confidence. "I know you will, Ethan," he said. "I believe in you."

Ethan left Noah's office with a renewed sense of purpose, a determination to not only succeed in his own career but to help Riley find her own path, to guide her towards a future where she could contribute her talents, her skills, and her unique perspective to the world. He knew it wouldn't be easy, but he was ready for the challenge. He was ready to be a leader, a mentor, a friend. He was ready to make a difference.

He returned to his desk, his mind buzzing with ideas, his heart filled with a newfound determination. He would find a way to connect with Riley, to break through her shell of indifference, to ignite the spark of passion and purpose that he knew lay dormant within her. He would show her the beauty of hard work, the satisfaction of accomplishment, the joy of collaboration. He would help her discover the leader within herself, the one who could make a difference, who could leave the world a little bit better than she found it.

He would prove to Noah, to the team, and to himself that he was more than just a creative mind with a knack for problem-solving. He was a leader, a mentor, a force for positive change. And he was ready to take on this new challenge, even if it meant facing a tidal wave of teenage angst and entitlement. He was ready to help Riley find her place in the world, to guide her towards a future where she could shine, where she could make her mark, where she could become the best version of herself.

CHAPTER XXII

# The Mentorship Challenge

The weight of responsibility settled on Ethan's shoulders like an unwelcome guest, a heavy cloak that stifled his usual enthusiasm. He paced his small apartment, the worn floorboards groaning beneath his restless steps, each step a heavy thud that mirrored the anxiety pounding in his chest. Riley. The governor's daughter. The newest addition to the Operations team. And the embodiment of everything he'd been trying to overcome – apathy, entitlement, and a complete disregard for the rules and expectations of the workplace.

"How am I supposed to mentor this?" he muttered to the empty room, his voice echoing off the bare walls, a hollow sound that mirrored the emptiness he felt inside. He could practically see Noah's disappointed frown, hear his curt dismissal, "Ethan, I expected better from you." The thought sent a shiver down his spine, a cold wave of fear washing over him. He couldn't fail Noah, not again. Not after everything he'd done to prove himself, to earn his trust, to show him that he was more than just a rookie with a knack for social media.

He'd tried. He really had. He'd tried to be patient, to be understanding, to channel the wisdom he'd gleaned from Noah and Mila about mentorship and leadership. He'd even dug out his old college textbooks on organizational behavior, their pages filled with underlined passages and scribbled notes, hoping for some forgotten nugget of wisdom that would unlock the secrets to motivating the seemingly unmotivated. He'd spent hours researching different leadership styles, different communication techniques, different motivational strategies, his mind a whirlwind of theories and concepts, his desk a battlefield of sticky notes and crumpled papers.

But Riley's nonchalance was a constant test, a challenge to his every carefully cultivated instinct. Every fiber of his being, honed by months of striving for excellence, of pushing himself to meet Noah's exacting standards, screamed in protest against Riley's casual disregard for the very foundations of their work. It was like trying to build a house on quicksand, the foundation constantly shifting, the structure threatening to collapse at any moment.

"Okay, Riley," he'd say, his voice a forced chirpiness that grated on his own ears, the words sticking in his throat like a mouthful of dry toast. "Let's review the data migration plan again. I want to make sure you understand the importance of accuracy and attention to detail. Every data point, every connection, every validation rule – it all matters. It all contributes to the bigger picture, to the success of the project, to the satisfaction of our clients."

He'd lay out the plan before her, the spreadsheets and diagrams a testament to the meticulous planning and preparation that had gone into this project. He'd explain the intricacies of the data migration process, the delicate dance of transferring information from one system to another, the potential pitfalls and challenges that lay ahead. He'd emphasize the importance of accuracy, of ensuring that every piece of data was validated, verified, and meticulously checked.

But Riley would just sigh dramatically, her eyes glazing over, her fingers resuming their relentless dance across her phone screen, the tapping a rhythmic counterpoint to his earnest explanations. "Ugh, fine," she'd mumble, her voice dripping with boredom and disdain, as if he were forcing her to watch paint dry. "But can we at least get some coffee first? I'm, like, totally not feeling this right now."

Ethan's jaw would clench, his patience wearing thin. He'd try to explain the importance of the project, the impact it could have on the company, on their clients, on their own careers. He'd paint a vivid picture of the future, of streamlined workflows, of happy clients, of promotions and bonuses raining down upon them like confetti. But his words seemed to fall on deaf ears, his passion met with a blank stare, his enthusiasm extinguished by her indifference.

"It's just a data migration project," she'd say, her voice flat, devoid of any discernible interest or motivation. "Why are you so stressed about it? It's not like it's going to change the world."

And that's when the frustration would bubble over, the carefully constructed dam of his patience cracking under the pressure of her apathy.

"It's not 'just' anything, Riley!" he'd snap, his voice rising in pitch, his hands clenching into fists. "This project is the foundation for the entire company's digital transformation. It's the key to unlocking new markets, to expanding our reach, to securing our future. It's about innovation, efficiency, and creating a better experience for our clients. It's about making a difference, damn it!"

He'd pace the room, his frustration growing with each step, his voice echoing off the walls, his words a desperate plea for her to understand, to engage, to care.

"Don't you get it, Riley?" he'd plead, his voice cracking with a mixture of anger and despair. "This isn't just about numbers and spreadsheets. It's about people. It's about making their lives easier, about helping them achieve their goals, about contributing to something bigger than ourselves. It's about making a positive impact on the world."

But Riley would just stare at him, her eyes wide with feigned innocence, a smirk playing on her lips. "Okay, boomer," she'd drawl, the dismissive label a stinging reminder of the generational divide that seemed to separate them, despite their shared age.

Ethan would grit his teeth, the anger and frustration threatening to consume him. He wanted to shake her, to scream at her, to force her to see the world through his eyes, to understand the passion, the dedication, the sheer effort that he poured into his work. But he knew that wouldn't work. He had to find another way, a way to connect with her, to inspire her, to awaken the potential that he knew lay dormant within her.

He tried different tactics. He tried appealing to her ambition, dangling the carrot of career advancement, painting a picture of her future self as a powerful executive, leading teams, making decisions, and raking in the big bucks. He'd weave tales of successful entrepreneurs, of young innovators who had disrupted industries and changed the world with their ideas and their drive.

He tried sparking her curiosity, emphasizing the innovative aspects of the data migration process, the cutting-edge technology they were using, the impact it could have on the industry. He'd regale her with stories of technological breakthroughs, of the power of data to transform businesses, to solve problems, to create a better future.

He even tried appealing to her sense of social responsibility, explaining how the project could improve the lives of their clients, could make a difference in the world, could contribute to a brighter future for all. He'd share examples of companies that were using technology to address social issues, to promote sustainability, to create a more equitable and just society.

But nothing seemed to work. Riley remained unmoved, her apathy a seemingly impenetrable fortress. Ethan began to doubt himself, his abilities as a mentor, his leadership potential. Was he simply not cut out for this? Was he too young, too inexperienced, too idealistic to handle the challenges of guiding someone like Riley? Was he, in fact, turning into Noah, the stern taskmaster, the enforcer of rules and deadlines, the one who sucked the joy out of everything?

The thought sent a shiver down his spine. He didn't want to be Noah. He wanted to be the kind of leader who inspired, who motivated, who brought out the best in people. But how could he do that when faced with someone who seemed determined to resist every effort, to reject every challenge, to wallow in a pool of apathy and entitlement?

He confided his frustrations to Mila one afternoon, seeking her wisdom, her guidance, her reassurance. He found her in the break room, her ever-present tumbler in hand, her eyes sparkling with a mix of amusement and empathy as he poured out his woes.

"I don't know what to do, Mila," he confessed, his voice laced with a hint of desperation. "I'm failing. I can't seem to reach her, to motivate her, to inspire her. It's like trying to teach a cat to fetch – it's just not in their nature."

Mila chuckled softly, her understanding gaze a comforting balm against his raw frustration. "Ethan," she said gently, "you're not failing. You're learning. And learning isn't always easy. It's messy, it's frustrating, and it often feels like you're taking one step forward and two steps back. But you're making progress, even if you can't see it yet."

She paused, her gaze meeting his, her voice firm and reassuring. "Don't give up on Riley, Ethan. She needs you. She needs someone to believe in her, to challenge her, to guide her. You have the potential to be that person for her, to help her discover the spark within herself, the passion that's waiting to be ignited."

Ethan nodded, his heart lifting slightly. Mila's words were a lifeline, a beacon of hope in the midst of his uncertainty. He wasn't alone in this. He had Mila, he had Noah, he had the team. And together, they would find a way to reach Riley, to help her find her place, to guide her towards a brighter future.

He returned to his desk, his resolve renewed, his determination strengthened. He would try again, he would find a new approach, he would break through Riley's apathy and awaken the potential that he knew lay dormant within her. He wouldn't give up, not on Riley, not on himself, not on the belief that everyone, even the most seemingly unmotivated and entitled, had the capacity for growth, for change, for greatness.

He spent the next few days observing Riley, trying to understand her, to decipher the code that lay beneath her indifference. He watched her interactions with the team, her body language, her subtle cues, her fleeting expressions. He listened to her conversations, her tone of voice, her choice of words, her underlying messages. He studied her work, her approach to tasks, her strengths and weaknesses, her patterns of behavior.

He started to see a different Riley, a more complex and nuanced individual than the one-dimensional stereotype he'd initially perceived. He saw glimpses of insecurity beneath her bravado, hints of vulnerability masked by her nonchalance, flickers of intelligence hidden behind her boredom. He saw a young woman who was lost, who was searching for her place in the world, who was afraid of failing, of not living up to the expectations that had been placed upon her.

He started to tailor his approach, adapting his communication style, adjusting his expectations, experimenting with different strategies to engage her, to challenge her, to inspire her. He shared his own experiences, his struggles, his triumphs, his failures, hoping to connect with her on a personal level, to show her that he understood, that he cared, that he believed in her.

He challenged her assumptions, questioned her apathy, pushed her to think critically, to engage with the work, to contribute her unique perspective. He'd ask her probing questions, "Why do you think this process is designed this way? What are the potential consequences of not following the protocol? How could we improve this system to make it more efficient?" He'd challenge her to think beyond the surface, to delve deeper into the "why" behind the "what."

He encouraged her to take ownership of her tasks, to take pride in her accomplishments, to see the value in her contributions to the team. He'd celebrate her small victories, acknowledge her efforts, and provide constructive feedback that focused on her growth and development.

And slowly, gradually, he began to see a shift in Riley's demeanor. The eye rolls became less frequent, the sighs less dramatic, the "whatever" replaced by a tentative "okay." She started to participate in discussions, to offer her own ideas, to ask questions, to show a flicker of interest in the project, in the team, in the company.

Ethan's heart soared with each small victory, each subtle sign of progress. He was making a difference, he was helping Riley, he was fulfilling his role as a mentor, a leader, a friend. And as he watched her grow, he realized that he was growing too, learning, evolving, becoming a better version of himself.

He was learning the patience that Noah had shown him, the understanding that Mila had offered him, the empathy that had allowed him to connect with Riley on a deeper level. He was learning to see beyond the surface, to recognize the potential that lay hidden within each individual, to inspire and empower others to become the best versions of themselves.

He was becoming the leader he was meant to be, the one who could guide, who could support, who could inspire. And as he looked at Riley, her eyes now shining with a newfound spark of interest and engagement, he knew that he had found his purpose, his calling, his place in the world.

## CHAPTER XXIII

# A Breakthrough Moment

The air in the office crackled with a nervous energy that had nothing to do with the approaching deadline. Ethan could feel it in the tense shoulders of his teammates, in the hushed whispers that replaced the usual banter, in the way their fingers flew across their keyboards with a frantic urgency that bordered on desperation. The Peterson account, a major client that had been teetering on the brink of disaster just a few weeks ago, was once again hanging in the balance, its fate dangling precariously over the abyss of failure.

The problem? A critical system malfunction that threatened to derail the entire data migration process, a catastrophic failure that could send shockwaves through the company, jeopardizing their reputation, their client relationships, and their financial stability. Ethan, his stomach churning with a familiar mix of anxiety and determination, a cocktail of emotions that had become his constant companion in the pressure cooker of SynergyWorks, huddled with Riley and Megan in a cramped conference room, the whiteboard a canvas for their frantic brainstorming session, a battlefield of ideas and anxieties.

"We've tried everything," Megan said, her voice laced with frustration, her usually calm demeanor cracking under the pressure, the strain evident in the lines etched around her eyes, the tightness in her jaw, the way her fingers drummed a restless rhythm against the table. "The system's throwing error messages we've never seen before. It's like it's deliberately trying to sabotage us, like it has a mind of its own and a vendetta against our success."

Riley, her phone abandoned on the table for once, its usual siren song of social media notifications silenced, her eyes fixed on the complex diagrams and code snippets scrawled across the whiteboard, chewed on her lip, her brow furrowed in concentration. The bored, dismissive expression that usually adorned her face had been replaced by a look of focus, of engagement, of a mind grappling with a challenge that demanded her full attention.

"Maybe it's a compatibility issue?" she suggested, her voice hesitant, a flicker of uncertainty in her eyes, a hint of vulnerability that surprised

Ethan. "Something in the legacy system that's conflicting with the new platform? Like, maybe they're speaking different languages, and the translation's getting lost somewhere in the digital ether?"

Ethan, his mind racing, sifting through the layers of complexity, the intricate web of connections and dependencies that made up the data migration process, considered the possibility. "It's worth exploring," he said, his voice regaining its usual confidence, the leadership role settling comfortably on his shoulders, the weight of responsibility a familiar burden that he now carried with a newfound ease. "But we need to be systematic. We need to isolate the variables, test the connections, and identify the root cause. We can't afford to waste time chasing dead ends, barking up the wrong digital trees."

He turned to Megan, his gaze seeking her expertise, her experience, the wisdom she'd accumulated over years of navigating the treacherous waters of the tech world. "Megan, can you pull up the system logs? Let's see if we can pinpoint the exact moment when the errors started occurring, the digital equivalent of a crime scene investigation."

Megan nodded, her fingers flying across her keyboard, her eyes scanning the screen with a focused intensity that spoke of years of experience, of countless hours spent deciphering the cryptic language of code and data. "Got it," she said, her voice regaining its usual calm efficiency, the reassuring tone of a seasoned professional who had weathered many storms. "The errors started appearing around 2:30 yesterday afternoon. Right after we implemented the latest batch of updates."

Ethan's mind raced, connecting the dots, the pieces of the puzzle falling into place with a satisfying click. "The updates," he muttered, his eyes widening with a sudden realization, a spark of intuition igniting in his mind. "Riley, didn't you handle those updates?"

Riley's face flushed, a wave of defensiveness washing over her, her eyes hardening, her voice taking on a defensive edge. "Yeah, so? I followed the protocols, I double-checked the code, I—"

"Did you test them?" Ethan interrupted, his voice sharp, his patience wearing thin, the frustration he'd been suppressing bubbling to the surface. "Did you run simulations? Did you consider the potential impact on the legacy system? Did you think about the consequences of your actions, the ripple effects that a single mistake could have on the entire project, on the company, on our clients?"

Noah, who had been silently observing the exchange, his expression unreadable, his mind assessing the situation, the dynamics between his team members, the potential fallout of this crisis, finally spoke, his voice cutting through the tension like a knife.

"Riley," he said, his tone sharp, his disapproval evident, "Ethan is leading this project. You need to follow his instructions, his guidance. And you need to understand that in Operations, there is no room for assumptions, for shortcuts, for carelessness. We deal with critical data, with sensitive information, with the lifeblood of our clients' businesses. We cannot afford to make mistakes."

Megan, her loyalty to Noah and her respect for the hierarchy overriding her usual support for her team members, chimed in, her voice firm, her gaze fixed on Riley. "Noah's right, Riley. You need to be more diligent, more thorough, more accountable for your actions. This isn't a game. This is our livelihood, our reputation, our future."

Riley's gaze dropped to the table, her fingers fidgeting with the edge of her notebook, her usual bravado crumbling under the combined weight of Noah and Megan's reprimands. The defiance in her eyes flickered and died, replaced by a flicker of shame, a hint of insecurity that she'd never allowed herself to show before.

But Ethan, seeing the vulnerability beneath her facade, the fear that mirrored his own anxieties, felt a surge of protectiveness, an unexpected urge to defend her, to shield her from the harshness of their judgment.

"Hold on a second," he said, his voice firm, his gaze meeting Noah's, a challenge in his eyes. "Riley's suggestion about a compatibility issue is worth exploring. It's possible that there's a conflict between the legacy system and the new platform that we haven't identified yet. We need to investigate that possibility before we jump to conclusions and start assigning blame."

He turned to Riley, his voice softening, his gaze conveying a message of support and encouragement. "Riley, I appreciate you bringing that up. It's a valid point, and we need to investigate it thoroughly. But next time, please make sure to communicate your concerns more clearly, to explain your reasoning, and to offer solutions, not just suggestions. We're a team, and we need to work together, to support each other, to learn from each other."

Riley's eyes widened, surprise and gratitude mingling in their depths. No one had ever defended her before, not in the workplace, not in her family, not in her entire life. She'd always been the governor's daughter, the one who was given everything, the one who was expected to succeed without effort, the one who was never challenged, never questioned, never held accountable.

And here was Ethan, this young man who had once seemed so eager to please, so desperate for approval, now standing up for her, defending her, believing in her. A warmth spread through her chest, a feeling she'd never experienced before, a sense of connection, of belonging, of being seen and valued for who she was, not just for who her father was.

"Thanks, Ethan," she mumbled, her voice barely a whisper, her eyes fixed on her hands, the carefully manicured nails suddenly seeming frivolous and insignificant.

"No problem, Riley," Ethan replied, his smile genuine, his confidence bolstered by the unexpected surge of protectiveness he felt towards this young woman who had challenged him, frustrated him, and ultimately, surprised him.

He turned back to Noah and Megan, his gaze steady, his voice firm. "Let's investigate this compatibility issue. Riley, you're with me. Megan, can you gather the relevant documentation on the legacy system?"

Noah and Megan exchanged glances, a silent acknowledgment of the shift in dynamics, the unexpected alliance that had formed between Ethan and Riley. They nodded, their expressions softening, their trust in Ethan's leadership reinforced by his willingness to defend his teammate, to see beyond her flaws, to recognize her potential.

The investigation began, the team working together with a renewed focus, their energy fueled by a combination of adrenaline, determination, and a newfound sense of unity. Ethan and Riley, their initial friction replaced by a tentative partnership, delved into the intricacies of the legacy system, their contrasting approaches complementing each other, their combined efforts creating a synergy that was greater than the sum of their parts.

And as they worked, they talked, they shared ideas, they challenged each other's assumptions, they learned from each other. Ethan, with his passion for innovation and his willingness to think outside the box, pushed Riley to question the status quo, to explore new possibilities, to see the world beyond the rigid confines of rules and protocols. Riley, with her meticulous attention to detail and her knowledge of the company's systems, helped Ethan to ground his ideas in reality, to ensure that his solutions were not just creative, but also practical and effective.

The hours flew by, the tension in the room gradually easing, replaced by a sense of camaraderie, a shared purpose, a growing respect for each other's strengths and perspectives. And as the sun began to set, casting long shadows across the office, they finally found it – the source of the error, a subtle incompatibility between the legacy system and the new platform, a hidden conflict that had been overlooked in the initial analysis.

A wave of relief washed over the team, followed by a surge of elation, a shared sense of accomplishment that transcended their individual roles, their generational differences, their personal challenges. They had faced a crisis, they had worked together, and they had emerged victorious.

And in that moment, Ethan realized that he had not only helped to save the project, he had also helped to save Riley. He had shown her the value of teamwork, the power of collaboration, the satisfaction of contributing to something bigger than herself. He had helped her to discover her own potential, to find her place in the world, to become the best version of herself.

And as he looked at Riley, her eyes shining with a newfound confidence, her smile genuine and bright, he knew that he had found his own place, his own purpose, his own path to greatness.

## CHAPTER XXIV

# Beyond Titles and Expectations

The break room hummed with the usual midday symphony – the clatter of mugs, the whir of the microwave, the low murmur of conversations punctuated by bursts of laughter. Ethan, perched on a stool by the counter, nursed a lukewarm coffee, his gaze drifting towards the window, the cityscape a blur of motion and ambition. He was still buzzing from the adrenaline rush of the previous day, the thrill of solving the Peterson crisis, the satisfaction of seeing Riley step up and contribute her skills to the team's success.

He hadn't expected that. He'd expected resistance, apathy, a continuation of the entitled nonchalance that had become her trademark. But Riley had surprised him. She'd shown a spark of intelligence, a willingness to learn, a dedication to the task at hand that had caught him off guard. And in the midst of the chaos, a connection had formed, a bridge built between two seemingly disparate worlds.

He felt a tap on his shoulder and turned to see Riley standing beside him, her usual casual attire replaced by a surprisingly professional blouse and a pair of neatly pressed slacks. Her hair, usually a mess of tangled waves, was pulled back into a sleek ponytail, her face scrubbed clean of makeup, revealing a vulnerability that Ethan hadn't noticed before.

"Hey," she said, her voice softer than usual, a hint of uncertainty in her tone. "Can we talk?"

Ethan nodded, surprised but intrigued. "Sure," he said, gesturing towards an empty table by the window. "Let's grab a seat."

They settled into the worn chairs, the silence between them a comfortable contrast to the bustling energy of the break room. Riley fidgeted with the strap of her bag, her gaze fixed on the swirling patterns of the linoleum floor, her usual confidence replaced by a quiet nervousness that made Ethan's heart ache.

"I just wanted to say thanks," she began, her voice barely a whisper, the words catching in her throat. "For yesterday. For believing in me, for defending me, for... seeing me."

Ethan's heart softened. He saw in Riley's vulnerability a reflection of his own struggles, his own insecurities, his own desperate need for acceptance and validation. He saw a young woman who was lost, who was searching for her place in the world, who was afraid of failing, of not living up to the expectations that had been placed upon her.

"You're welcome, Riley," he said, his voice gentle, reassuring. "We all make mistakes. The important thing is that we learn from them. And I know you will. You're smart, you're capable, and you have the potential to be great. Don't let anyone tell you otherwise, not even yourself."

Riley's eyes met his, a flicker of gratitude and a newfound determination shining in their depths. "I've never had anyone say that to me before," she confessed, her voice cracking with emotion. "Not really. Everyone always just saw me as the governor's daughter, the one who had it all, the one who didn't have to work for anything."

She paused, her gaze drifting towards the window, the cityscape a blur of motion and ambition, a world that had always seemed both accessible and unattainable to her. "I used to think that was a good thing," she continued, her voice laced with a hint of bitterness. "I was proud of my dad, of his success, of the doors it opened for me. I thought it meant I didn't have to struggle, that I could just coast through life, that everything would be handed to me on a silver platter."

She let out a hollow laugh, the sound devoid of humor. "But yesterday, when I saw the look on Noah's face, the disappointment, the disapproval... it was like a slap in the face. For the first time, I realized that I wasn't just Riley, the governor's daughter. I was Riley, the Operations intern, the one who had screwed up, the one who had let the team down."

She looked at Ethan, her eyes filled with a raw honesty that he hadn't seen before. "And you know what? It felt... liberating. Terrifying, but also liberating. Because for the first time, I felt like I was being seen for who I was, not for who my father was. I felt like I had a chance to prove myself, to earn my place, to make my own mark on the world."

Ethan nodded, his heart swelling with empathy and admiration. He understood the struggle, the desire to break free from the expectations and labels that others placed upon you, to forge your own path, to define your own identity.

"It's not easy," he said, his voice soft but firm. "But it's worth it. Trust me, Riley, there's nothing more satisfying than knowing you've earned your place, that you've achieved something on your own merits, that you're not just living in someone else's shadow."

Riley's lips curved into a genuine smile, the first one Ethan had seen from her that wasn't laced with cynicism or boredom. "I believe you, Ethan," she said, her voice filled with a newfound confidence. "And I'm ready to work for it. I'm ready to prove myself, to you, to Noah, to the team, and most importantly, to myself."

Ethan grinned, his own confidence bolstered by her determination. "That's the spirit, Riley," he said. "And hey, if you ever need any help, any guidance, any support, I'm here for you. We're in this together."

Riley's smile widened, her eyes sparkling with gratitude. "Thanks, Ethan," she said. "I appreciate that."

They sat in silence for a moment, the comfortable quiet a testament to the newfound bond that had formed between them, the shared understanding that transcended their differences, their backgrounds, their initial perceptions of each other.

"So," Ethan said finally, breaking the silence with a playful grin, "what do you say we get back to work and show those data servers who's boss?"

Riley laughed, the sound light and carefree, a melody that filled the room with a sense of hope and optimism. "Let's do it, Ethan," she said, her voice filled with a newfound energy and enthusiasm. "Let's show them what we're made of."

As they left the break room, their shoulders squared, their steps purposeful, Ethan couldn't help but feel a surge of excitement for the future, for the challenges that lay ahead, for the opportunity to work alongside Riley, to guide her, to support her, to watch her grow and evolve into the amazing woman he knew she could be.

He had a feeling that this partnership, this unexpected friendship, was going to be more than just a professional collaboration. It was going to be a journey of discovery, a shared adventure, a testament to the power of human connection and the transformative potential of mentorship. And he was ready for it, eager to embrace the challenges, the triumphs, and the lessons that awaited them.

CHAPTER XXV

# The Price of Perfection

The email arrived on a Tuesday morning, nestled amongst the usual deluge of meeting invites, project updates, and automated reminders. Ethan scanned the subject line – "Noah Out Sick" – and felt a jolt of surprise, a ripple of unease spreading through his chest. Noah? Sick? The man was practically a machine, a tireless force of nature who seemed impervious to the ailments that plagued mere mortals.

Ethan's mind raced, replaying the events of the past few weeks, the late nights, the tense meetings, the relentless pressure that Noah had been under. He thought about the conversation they'd had after the Peterson crisis, the vulnerability Noah had revealed, the confession of his own struggles with work-life balance, the promise to try to do better.

Had he pushed Noah too far? Ethan wondered, a wave of guilt washing over him. Had his own challenges, his own questions, his own insistence on a more balanced approach to work, triggered something in Noah, a breaking point that had finally shattered the illusion of invincibility?

He couldn't shake the feeling that he was somehow responsible, that his own desire for a life beyond spreadsheets and deadlines had inadvertently pushed Noah over the edge. He felt a surge of empathy for his boss, the man who had once seemed so distant, so intimidating, now revealed as a flawed and vulnerable human being, just like him.

Ethan's own anxieties about work-life balance had been growing lately. He'd been feeling the pressure of deadlines, the weight of expectations, the constant need to prove himself. He'd been working late nights, skipping meals, and neglecting his relationships, all in the pursuit of success, of recognition, of validation.

But seeing Noah, the man who embodied the very essence of dedication and work ethic, now lying sick and vulnerable in his bed, made Ethan question the price of perfection, the cost of sacrificing everything for the sake of a career.

He thought about his own generation, the Gen Zers who were entering the workforce with a different set of values, a different set of priorities. They weren't just looking for a job, a paycheck, a career ladder to climb. They were looking for meaning, for purpose, for a way to make a difference in the world, to leave their mark, to create a life that was both fulfilling and impactful.

They weren't afraid to question the status quo, to challenge the norms, to push for change. They weren't afraid to prioritize their personal lives, their passions, their relationships, their mental and physical well-being. They weren't afraid to say no to the endless demands of the corporate world, to set boundaries, to create a life that was truly their own.

Ethan, caught between these two worlds, the world of his parents, of Noah, of the traditional workplace, and the world of his peers, of his generation, of the future he wanted to create, felt a growing sense of dissonance, a conflict between the expectations that had been placed upon him and the desires that burned within him.

He wanted to succeed, to make a difference, to leave his mark on the world. But he also wanted to live, to experience, to enjoy the journey, to create a life that was rich and fulfilling, not just a means to an end.

He looked at Noah, his face pale and drawn, his eyes closed in restless sleep, and he couldn't help but wonder if this was the price of perfection, the cost of sacrificing everything for the sake of a career.

Ethan couldn't focus on his work. The spreadsheets blurred before his eyes, the code refused to cooperate, and the usual hum of the office seemed to mock his inability to concentrate. He paced his cubicle, his restless energy a stark contrast to the quiet efficiency of his colleagues, his mind a whirlwind of worry and self-recrimination.

Finally, unable to bear the uncertainty any longer, he grabbed his jacket and headed out the door, ignoring the surprised glances of his coworkers. He hailed a cab, the city lights a blur through the window as he sped towards Noah's apartment, his anxiety growing with each passing block.

He arrived at the familiar building, remembering the team dinner they'd had there weeks ago, the warmth of the gathering, the camaraderie that had surprised him. He'd seen a different side of Noah that night, a more relaxed and approachable side, a glimpse of the man behind the manager.

Ethan pressed the buzzer, a familiar nervousness fluttering in his stomach. The door buzzed open, and he stepped inside, the hallway dimly lit, the air heavy with a silence that spoke of Noah's absence. He followed the sound of a cough to the bedroom, where he found Noah propped up in bed, his face pale, his eyes glazed with fever. The usually meticulous Noah was surrounded by a chaotic jumble of tissues, medicine bottles, and half-empty water glasses.

"Noah?" Ethan said softly, his voice filled with concern. "It's Ethan. I heard you were sick, and I wanted to check on you."

Noah's eyes fluttered open, a flicker of surprise crossing his face. "Ethan? What are you doing here?" he croaked, his voice hoarse and weak.

"I was worried about you," Ethan admitted, his voice softening. "You haven't been yourself lately. You've been pushing yourself too hard, working late nights, skipping meals, neglecting your health."

Noah sighed, a weary sound that spoke of years of accumulated stress and exhaustion. "I'm fine, Ethan," he said, his voice barely a whisper. "Just a little bug. I'll be back in the office tomorrow."

Ethan shook his head, his concern deepening. "No, you won't," he said firmly. "You need to rest, Noah. You need to take care of yourself. You can't keep burning the candle at both ends. It's not sustainable."

Noah's gaze drifted towards the window, the city lights a distant blur through the rain-streaked glass. "I don't know how to do anything else, Ethan," he confessed, his voice laced with a vulnerability that Ethan had rarely seen before. "Work is all I have. It's my identity, my purpose, my validation."

Ethan's heart ached for Noah, the man who had always seemed so strong, so in control, now revealing a fragility that mirrored his own insecurities. He sat down on the edge of the bed, his gaze meeting Noah's, his voice filled with empathy and understanding.

"Noah," he said gently, "there's more to life than work. There's family, friends, passions, experiences. There's a whole world out there waiting to be explored, waiting to be enjoyed. You don't have to sacrifice your life for your career. You can have both. You deserve both."

Noah's eyes widened, a flicker of hope igniting in their depths. Ethan's words were like a lifeline, a beacon of light in the darkness that had enveloped him. He'd been so caught up in the relentless pursuit of success, the endless cycle of deadlines and deliverables, that he'd forgotten the simple joys of life, the things that truly mattered.

He thought about his neglected hobbies, the guitar gathering dust in the corner, the unread books piled on his shelves, the long-forgotten dreams of traveling the world, of exploring new cultures, of experiencing life beyond the confines of his work.

He thought about his estranged family, the strained relationships that had withered under the weight of his ambition, the missed birthdays, the unanswered phone calls, the growing distance that separated him from the people who loved him.

"I haven't spoken to my sister in months," he confessed, his voice cracking with regret. "We used to be so close, but now... I don't even know what to say to her. I've let her down, Ethan. I've let everyone down."

Ethan listened patiently, his heart aching for Noah, the man who had always seemed so invincible, now revealing the deep wounds that his ambition had inflicted on his personal life.

"It's not too late, Noah," Ethan said, his voice filled with a gentle conviction. "You can still rebuild those relationships, reconnect with the people you love, rediscover the passions that make you feel alive. It's not going to be easy, but it's worth it. Trust me, I know."

Ethan shared his own struggles with balancing work and life, his anxieties about meeting expectations, his fear of disappointing those he cared about. He talked about the support he'd received from his parents, from Mila, from Lauren, and how their encouragement had helped him to find a healthier balance, to prioritize his well-being, to pursue his passions.

"It's a journey, Noah," he said, his voice filled with empathy and understanding. "And it's not one you have to take alone. We're all here for you, your team, your friends, your family. We want you to be happy, Noah. We want you to thrive, not just survive."

Noah's eyes glistened with unshed tears, his heart swelling with gratitude for Ethan's unexpected kindness, his unwavering support. He had never allowed himself to be vulnerable, to show weakness, to ask for help. But now, in the quiet intimacy of his bedroom, with the rain drumming a soothing rhythm against the windowpanes, he felt a sense of release, a freedom from the shackles of his own self-imposed expectations.

"Thank you, Ethan," he whispered, his voice thick with emotion. "For reminding me what truly matters."

Ethan smiled, his heart swelling with hope. He knew it wouldn't be easy for Noah to break free from the patterns of a lifetime, to rewire the ingrained habits that had defined his existence. But he also knew that Noah was capable of change, that he had the strength and the resilience to create a new path, a path that led towards a more balanced, fulfilling, and meaningful life.

"I'm here for you, Noah," Ethan said, his voice firm and reassuring. "We'll figure it out together. We'll find a way to balance the work with the life, the ambition with the joy, the success with the fulfillment."

Noah's lips curved into a grateful smile, the lines around his eyes softening, the tension in his shoulders easing. He reached out, his hand grasping Ethan's, a silent gesture of gratitude and trust.

"Thank you, Ethan," he said, his voice filled with emotion. "For reminding me what truly matters."

Ethan squeezed his hand, his gaze meeting Noah's, a silent promise of support and companionship. They sat in silence for a moment, the quiet hum of the city a comforting backdrop to their shared moment of vulnerability and connection.

And as the rain continued to fall outside, washing away the grime and the dust, cleansing the city, Ethan felt a sense of hope, a belief that even in the midst of chaos and uncertainty, there was always the possibility of renewal, of growth, of transformation. He knew that Noah had a long road ahead of him, but he also knew that Noah wasn't alone. He had Ethan, he had Mila, he had the team, and he had the potential to create a life that was both successful and fulfilling, a life that honored his values, his passions, and his dreams.

As Ethan stood to leave, Noah's voice stopped him. "Ethan," he said, his voice hoarse but filled with a newfound clarity, "thank you for coming. It means more than you know."

Ethan smiled, his heart warmed by Noah's sincerity. "Anytime, Noah," he said. "Get some rest. We need you back in the office, but we need you healthy and happy, not just productive."

Noah nodded, a genuine smile gracing his lips. "I'll try," he said, his voice filled with a tentative hope.

Ethan left the apartment, the rain having stopped, the city lights shining brightly against the night sky. He walked with a newfound lightness in his step, his heart filled with a sense of purpose and optimism. He had faced his own anxieties, had confronted his fears, and had emerged stronger, more resilient, more compassionate. And he had helped Noah to do the same, to take the first step towards a more balanced and fulfilling life.

As he hailed a cab, the city lights reflecting in his eyes, Ethan couldn't help but smile. He was learning, he was growing, he was making a difference. And he knew, with a certainty that transcended words, that the journey was just beginning.

CHAPTER XXVI

# A New Dawn, A New Harmony

The office buzzed with a different kind of energy the following week. It wasn't just the usual hum of productivity, the clatter of keyboards, the murmur of conversations. There was a lightness in the air, a sense of relief, a collective exhale after the storm. The Peterson crisis had passed, the client appeased, the account secured. But the experience had left its mark, a subtle shift in the atmosphere, a newfound appreciation for the fragility of success, the importance of balance, the value of human connection. It was as if the team had gone through a collective trial by fire, emerging stronger, more united, their individual strengths forged into a collective resilience.

Ethan walked with a newfound confidence, his shoulders squared, his gaze steady, his steps purposeful. He'd faced his fears, had confronted his doubts, and had emerged stronger, more resilient, more certain of his place in the world. He'd proven himself, not just to Noah, to the team, to the company, but to himself. He was no longer just the rookie, the intern, the one who needed constant guidance and reassurance. He was Ethan, the problem-solver, the innovator, the leader. He was the one who had dared to question, to challenge, to push for a better way, and in doing so, had not only helped to save a crucial account but had also sparked a change in the very culture of the company.

He stopped by Noah's office, a tentative knock on the door a gesture of respect and concern, a habit he'd learned from Noah himself, a subtle acknowledgment of the boundaries that existed even within their newfound camaraderie.

"Come in," Noah's voice called out, the usual gruffness softened by a warmth that surprised Ethan, a hint of vulnerability that spoke of the transformation the man had undergone.

He pushed the door open, stepping into the familiar space, the air thick with the scent of old books and freshly brewed coffee, a comforting blend of intellectual curiosity and grounded energy. Noah sat at his desk, his gaze fixed on the cityscape beyond the window, the morning sun casting a warm glow on his face, highlighting the lines that had softened, the tension that had eased, replaced by a newfound serenity.

"How are you feeling, Noah?" Ethan asked, his voice filled with genuine concern, the question a testament to the bond that had formed between them, the friendship that had blossomed in the midst of adversity.

Noah turned, a smile gracing his lips, a sight that had become increasingly common in the past few days, a welcome change from the stoic mask he usually wore. "Better, Ethan," he said, his voice stronger, clearer, the weariness replaced by a newfound energy, a vibrancy that spoke of a rekindled passion for life. "Much better. Thanks for asking."

Ethan nodded, his gaze taking in the subtle changes in Noah's demeanor, the relaxed posture, the lightness in his eyes, the absence of the constant tension that had always seemed to cling to him like a shadow. He saw a man who was starting to rediscover himself, to shed the weight of his past, to embrace the possibilities of the future.

"I've been doing a lot of thinking," Noah continued, his gaze returning to the cityscape, the buildings now seeming less like imposing structures and more like symbols of possibility, of opportunity, of a world waiting to be explored. "About what you said, about work-life balance, about the importance of living, not just working."

He paused, his eyes meeting Ethan's, a flicker of gratitude and admiration in their depths. "You were right, Ethan. I've been living my life out of balance, sacrificing everything for the sake of my career, neglecting the things that truly matter - my family, my friends, my passions."

He took a deep breath, his shoulders relaxing further, the weight of years of accumulated stress seemingly lifting from his frame, leaving behind a sense of lightness, of freedom. "I'm going to change that, Ethan. I'm going to start living a more balanced life, a life that includes not just work, but also joy, connection, and fulfillment. I'm going to reconnect with my family, rekindle my passions, and rediscover the world outside the office."

Ethan's heart swelled with a mixture of pride and relief. He had made a difference. He had not only helped Noah to recover from his illness, but he had also inspired him to change, to grow, to embrace a new way of living. He had been the catalyst for a transformation that had not only benefited Noah, but had also rippled outward, affecting the entire team, the entire company, creating a more positive and fulfilling work environment.

"I'm proud of you, Noah," Ethan said, his voice filled with sincerity. "It takes courage to admit that you need to change, to step outside your comfort zone and embrace a new path."

Noah smiled, a genuine smile that reached his eyes, a smile that spoke of gratitude and newfound hope. "Thank you, Ethan," he said. "I couldn't have done it without you. You've been a true friend, a mentor, a guide. You've shown me the way."

Ethan's cheeks flushed with a warmth that spread through his entire being. He had never thought of himself as a mentor, as a guide, as someone who could inspire others to change. But now, seeing the impact he'd had on Noah, the man who had once seemed so invincible, so unapproachable, he realized that he had the power to make a difference, to influence those around him, to create a ripple effect that could extend far beyond the walls of the office.

"We've both learned a lot from each other, Noah," Ethan said, his voice filled with a quiet confidence. "You've taught me the value of discipline, of precision, of accountability. And I've hopefully shown you the importance of balance, of connection, of living a life that's not just about work, but about passion, purpose, and fulfillment."

Noah nodded, his gaze fixed on Ethan, a silent acknowledgment of the bond that had formed between them, the partnership that had been forged in the crucible of crisis, the friendship that had blossomed in the midst of adversity.

"I'm glad you're on my team, Ethan," he said, his voice filled with a sincerity that Ethan had rarely heard before. "You're a valuable asset, not just to the company, but to me personally. You've helped me to see the world in a new light, to rediscover the things that truly matter, to become a better version of myself."

Ethan's heart swelled with gratitude and a sense of belonging. He had found his place, his purpose, his tribe. He was no longer just an employee, a cog in the corporate machine. He was a valued member of a team, a friend, a mentor, a leader. And he was ready to embrace the challenges, the triumphs, and the lessons that lay ahead, knowing that he wasn't alone, that he had Noah, Mila, and the rest of the team by his side, supporting him, guiding him, and inspiring him to be the best version of himself.

Just then, Riley poked her head into the office, her usual nonchalance replaced by a hesitant smile. "Hey guys," she said, her voice softer than usual. "I'm having a little get-together at my place tonight. Just a casual thing, some music, some food, some drinks. You guys should come."

Noah's initial instinct was to decline. He had a stack of reports to review, emails to answer, and a presentation to prepare for Monday morning. But then he looked at Ethan, at the hopeful expression on his face, the eagerness in his eyes, and he remembered his own resolutions, his promise to himself to start living, to embrace the moments, to connect with the people who mattered.

"Sure, Riley," he said, surprising himself with his own spontaneity. "We'll be there."

Riley's smile widened, her eyes sparkling with gratitude. "Awesome! See you guys tonight!"

Ethan grinned, his heart filled with a sense of anticipation. He couldn't wait to see the look on everyone's faces when they discovered the hidden talents of their stoic boss.

**The Gathering**

Ethan blinked, momentarily stunned by the sheer opulence that greeted him as he stepped into Riley's apartment. He'd expected something... different. A typical Gen Z pad, maybe, with mismatched furniture, overflowing bookshelves, and posters of obscure bands plastered on the walls. But this? This was something else entirely.

The entryway alone was larger than his entire living room, the polished marble floor gleaming beneath a sparkling chandelier that looked like it belonged in a palace. A grand staircase swept upwards, disappearing into the shadows of the upper floor, its wrought-iron railing intricately crafted, a testament to the artistry of some long-dead blacksmith. Ethan's gaze swept over the plush velvet couches, the antique mahogany tables, the priceless artwork adorning the walls, each piece a masterpiece that whispered of wealth, privilege, and a history that Ethan could only dream of.

He followed the sound of music and laughter down a long hallway, his footsteps sinking into the thick Persian carpet, the silence punctuated by the clinking of glasses and the murmur of conversations. He emerged into a vast living room, the space bathed in the warm glow of strategically placed lamps and the soft flicker of a crackling fireplace. The room was a symphony of textures and colors, the plush velvet furniture contrasting with the rough-hewn stone fireplace, the vibrant tapestries adding a touch of bohemian flair to the otherwise classic décor.

But it wasn't the décor that caught Ethan's attention, it was the people. Not just his colleagues, who were scattered throughout the room, their faces relaxed and animated, their laughter echoing through the spacious apartment, but also the others, the strangers who moved with an air of quiet efficiency, catering to the guests' every need. There were waiters in crisp uniforms circulating with trays of hors d'oeuvres, their movements graceful and silent, their smiles impeccable. There was a bartender expertly mixing cocktails behind a gleaming mahogany bar, his hands a blur of motion as he poured and stirred, his creations a symphony of colors and flavors. And there was a woman in a starched white apron gliding through the room, clearing away empty glasses and plates, her presence as unobtrusive as a whisper.

Ethan's mind reeled. He'd never seen so many people working in a private residence before. It was like stepping into a scene from a movie, a glimpse into a world of privilege and luxury that he'd only ever imagined. He thought about his own modest apartment, the cramped kitchen, the overflowing laundry basket, the constant struggle to keep up with the demands of daily life. And then he looked at Riley, the governor's daughter, the one who had grown up surrounded by this kind of opulence, this effortless abundance, this army of silent servants catering to her every whim.

He couldn't help but feel a twinge of envy, a flicker of resentment. It wasn't fair. It wasn't right. Why did some people get to be born into this kind of privilege, while others had to struggle and strive for every inch of progress?

But then he remembered the conversation he'd had with Noah, the vulnerability he'd witnessed, the regret he'd heard in Noah's voice as he spoke of the sacrifices he'd made, the relationships he'd neglected, the life he'd missed out on in his relentless pursuit of success.

And Ethan realized that privilege wasn't always a blessing. It could be a burden, a gilded cage that trapped you in a world of expectations and obligations, that prevented you from experiencing the simple joys of life, the struggles that shaped you, the challenges that made you stronger.

He looked at Riley again, her face flushed with excitement, her eyes sparkling with a newfound joy as she chatted with her colleagues, her laughter echoing through the room, a melody of genuine happiness that Ethan hadn't heard from her before. And he realized that maybe, just maybe, this experience, this glimpse into a world beyond her privileged bubble, was exactly what she needed.

Maybe it was the catalyst for the change he'd been trying to inspire in her, the spark that would ignite her passion, her ambition, her desire to make her own mark on the world, not as the governor's daughter, but as Riley, the individual, the one with her own unique talents, her own dreams, her own path to forge.

And as he watched her interact with the team, her laughter mingling with theirs, her smile genuine and bright, Ethan felt a surge of hope, a belief that maybe, just maybe, he was making a difference, not just in Riley's life, but in his own as well.

The atmosphere at Riley's apartment was a stark contrast to the usual sterile environment of the office. The spacious living room, bathed in the warm glow of strategically placed lamps and the soft flicker of a crackling fireplace, buzzed with a relaxed energy that Ethan had rarely witnessed amongst his colleagues. The room was a symphony of textures and colors, the plush velvet furniture contrasting with the rough-hewn stone fireplace, the vibrant tapestries adding a touch of bohemian flair to the otherwise classic décor. Laughter and conversation flowed freely, mingling with the enticing aroma of gourmet snacks and the clinking of glasses.

Ethan, still slightly dazed by the opulence of his surroundings, found himself drawn to a corner of the room where a familiar melody drifted through the air. It was "Wonderwall" by Oasis, a classic rock anthem that evoked memories of family road trips and singalongs with his friends. He followed the sound, his curiosity piqued, his heart quickening with anticipation.

And then he saw him.

Noah.

Not the Noah he knew from the office, the stern, unyielding manager with his crisp suits and his meticulously organized desk. This Noah was different. He sat perched on a stool, his shoulders relaxed, his head tilted back slightly, his eyes closed as his fingers danced across the fretboard of an acoustic guitar, the worn wood gleaming softly beneath the dim light. The music flowed from him, a torrent of passion and energy that belied his usual stoic demeanor. He played with a skill that Ethan had never imagined, his fingers moving effortlessly across the strings, his voice soaring with the melody, the lyrics resonating with a raw emotion that sent shivers down Ethan's spine.

It was a revelation, a glimpse into a hidden world, a side of Noah that he had never seen before. The Noah who had once seemed so distant, so intimidating, was now revealed as a musician, an artist, a soul filled with passion and creativity.

The rest of the team, gathered around the makeshift stage, their faces a mixture of surprise and delight, echoed Ethan's astonishment. Mila, her ever-present tumbler in hand, let out a whoop of encouragement, her laughter filling the room with a contagious energy. "Go, Noah, go!" she yelled, her voice laced with a playful challenge. "Show these youngsters how it's done!"

Megan, her eyes wide with wonder, tapped her foot to the rhythm, a rare smile gracing her lips, her usual reserve melting away as she swayed to the music. Even Amir, the quietest member of the team, couldn't help but grin, his head bobbing in time with the beat.

And Riley, beaming with pride, her eyes sparkling with a newfound admiration for her boss, joined in on the chorus, her voice blending with Noah's in a harmonious duet that resonated through the apartment, creating a sense of unity, of connection, of shared joy.

Ethan watched the scene unfold, his heart swelling with a mix of emotions – surprise, admiration, gratitude, and a deep sense of belonging. He had found his place, his tribe, his family. And in this moment, surrounded by the warmth of friendship, the magic of music, and the shared laughter of his colleagues, he knew that he was exactly where he was meant to be.

Noah, lost in the music, his fingers flying across the fretboard, his voice soaring with the melody, felt a sense of freedom he hadn't experienced in years. The weight of responsibility, the pressure of expectations, the burden of leadership – it all melted away, replaced by the pure joy of creation, the exhilaration of self-expression, the connection to something deeper than himself.

He played song after song, his repertoire a surprising mix of 90s classics. "Smells Like Teen Spirit" by Nirvana had everyone headbanging, while "Losing My Religion" by R.E.M. had them singing along with a nostalgic fervor. He even threw in a soulful rendition of "Glycerine" by Bush, his voice cracking with emotion, the lyrics resonating with a depth that surprised even himself.

The room echoed with the sounds of a bygone era, the music transporting them back to a time of simpler pleasures, of carefree abandon, of shared experiences that had shaped their lives, their perspectives, their very identities. It was a time when the world felt full of possibilities, a time before the pressures of adulthood, the burdens of responsibility, the weight of expectations.

As the night wore on, the boundaries between boss and employee blurred, replaced by a sense of camaraderie, of shared humanity, of a connection that transcended their professional roles. They sang along, they danced, they laughed, they shared stories, they revealed their vulnerabilities, they forged bonds that would last a lifetime.

And in that moment, Ethan understood. He understood why Noah had pushed him so hard, why he had demanded so much, why he had held him to such a high standard. It wasn't about control, it wasn't about ego, it was about passion, about dedication, about the unwavering belief in the potential of those around him. It was about wanting Ethan to be the best version of himself, to shine as brightly as Noah knew he could.

And Ethan, in turn, had shown Noah the importance of balance, of connection, of living a life that was not just about work, but about passion, purpose, and fulfillment. He had helped Noah to rediscover the music that had once brought him joy, to reconnect with the part of himself that had been buried beneath the weight of responsibility and expectation.

They had learned from each other, had grown together, had become better versions of themselves through their shared experiences, their challenges, their triumphs. And as the night drew to a close, the last notes of "Closing Time" by Semisonic fading into the quiet hum of the city, they knew that they had found something truly special, a bond that would last a lifetime, a partnership that would shape not just their careers, but their lives.

CHAPTER XXVII

# The Power of Teamwork, The Echoes of Success

The air crackled with anticipation, a palpable energy that thrummed through the Operations department, a symphony of excitement and relief. The data migration project, a monumental undertaking that had tested the team's skills, their patience, and their ability to collaborate under pressure, was finally nearing completion. Weeks of late nights, fueled by caffeine and adrenaline; frantic troubleshooting sessions, where the whiteboard became a battleground of ideas and anxieties; and endless cups of coffee, their bitter taste a constant reminder of the challenges they faced – all of it had culminated in this moment, the final push towards the finish line.

Ethan, his eyes bloodshot but his spirit soaring, surveyed the scene with a mix of pride and exhaustion. He'd come a long way since his first days at SynergyWorks, the wide-eyed rookie who had stumbled through meetings, fumbled with spreadsheets, and struggled to keep up with Noah's demanding expectations. Now, he stood as a leader, a mentor, a driving force behind the team's success, his voice carrying weight, his opinions valued, his contributions recognized.

He'd learned to navigate the complexities of the corporate world, to decipher the cryptic language of spreadsheets and code, to translate the jargon of executives and engineers into a language that everyone could understand. He'd learned to balance his creative instincts with the discipline and precision required in Operations, to temper his enthusiasm with a healthy dose of pragmatism, to channel his energy into solutions, not just ideas. He'd learned to trust his colleagues, to delegate effectively, to leverage their strengths and compensate for their weaknesses, to build a team that was greater than the sum of its parts.

The data migration project had been a crucible, forging new bonds, testing old alliances, and revealing hidden strengths. Ethan had watched as Riley, the governor's daughter, had shed her shell of apathy and entitlement, her transformation a testament to his patient mentorship and her own innate desire to prove herself. He'd seen the spark of intelligence ignite in her eyes, the flicker of determination that replaced her usual boredom, the quiet confidence that blossomed as she mastered new skills and contributed her unique perspective to the team.

He'd seen Megan, the quiet and efficient workhorse, step up and take charge, her leadership skills blossoming under the pressure of the deadline. He'd witnessed her calm demeanor transform into a quiet force of authority, her voice gaining strength, her decisions becoming more decisive, her presence commanding respect and admiration.

And he'd witnessed Amir, the soft-spoken tech wizard, become a vocal advocate for his ideas, his confidence growing with each successful challenge. He'd seen the hesitant programmer blossom into a passionate problem-solver, his voice ringing with conviction, his ideas shaping the project's direction, his contributions essential to the team's success.

Even Noah, the stoic and demanding boss, had undergone a subtle shift. The lines on his face had softened, his smile had become more frequent, and his interactions with the team had taken on a new warmth and approachability. He'd learned to delegate, to trust, to let go of the reins and allow his team to shine, to recognize that leadership wasn't just about control and authority, but about empowering others, about fostering growth, about creating a space where everyone could contribute their unique talents and perspectives.

And now, as the final pieces of the project fell into place, the data flowing seamlessly from the old system to the new, the errors minimized, the risks mitigated, Ethan felt a surge of triumph, a shared victory that resonated through the entire team, a symphony of accomplishment that echoed through the office, a testament to their collective effort, their perseverance, their unwavering commitment to excellence.

"We did it!" Riley exclaimed, her voice filled with a jubilant energy that Ethan had rarely heard from her before, a genuine expression of joy that lit up her face, erasing the last vestiges of her former apathy. "We actually did it!"

Megan, her usual reserve cracking, let out a whoop of joy, her laughter echoing through the office, a sound that was both infectious and liberating. Amir, his face beaming with pride, gave Ethan a high-five, his silent approval speaking volumes, a gesture of camaraderie that transcended words.

And Noah, his eyes twinkling with a mixture of satisfaction and gratitude, approached Ethan, his hand outstretched, his usually stern expression softened by a warmth that spoke of a deeper connection, a newfound respect and appreciation for the young man who had challenged him, inspired him, and ultimately, helped him to become a better leader.

"Ethan," he said, his voice firm but warm, "congratulations. You and your team have done an outstanding job. This project was a challenge, but you rose to the occasion, you exceeded expectations, and you delivered results. I'm proud of you, Ethan. I'm proud of all of you."

Ethan's chest swelled with emotion, his heart filled with a sense of accomplishment that transcended the project itself. It was a victory not just for the team, but for the company, for the clients, for the future of SynergyWorks. And it was a victory for Ethan personally, a testament to his growth, his resilience, his ability to lead, to inspire, and to make a difference.

As the team gathered for a celebratory dinner that evening, the atmosphere was electric, the air thick with laughter, camaraderie, and a shared sense of accomplishment. Ethan, raising his glass in a toast, his gaze sweeping over the faces of his colleagues, his friends, his family, felt a surge of gratitude, a deep appreciation for the journey they had taken together, the challenges they had overcome, the bonds they had forged.

"To the team," he said, his voice filled with emotion, "to SynergyWorks, to the future, and to the power of teamwork."

The glasses clinked, the cheers echoed, and the room filled with a warmth that radiated from their shared victory, a warmth that promised a brighter future, a future where collaboration, communication, and mutual support would pave the way for even greater achievements.

**A Family Celebration**

The warmth of the victory lingered as Ethan made his way home that evening, the city lights blurring into a kaleidoscope of colors and emotions. He couldn't wait to share the news with his parents, to bask in their pride, to revel in their unwavering support.

He burst through the door, his excitement bubbling over, his voice echoing through the quiet house. "Mom! Dad! Guess what?"

His parents emerged from the living room, their faces etched with concern at his breathless entrance.

"Ethan? What's wrong? Are you alright?" his mother asked, her voice laced with worry.

Ethan laughed, a joyous sound that filled the room, dispelling their anxieties. "I'm more than alright, Mom. I'm amazing! We did it! We finished the data migration project, and it was a huge success! Noah even congratulated me, said I did an outstanding job!"

His parents' faces erupted in smiles, their eyes shining with pride and happiness. "Ethan, that's wonderful!" his mother exclaimed, pulling him into a warm embrace. "We're so proud of you!"

His father clapped him on the shoulder, his grip firm and reassuring. "Well done, son. You've come a long way. We always knew you had it in you."

Ethan basked in their praise, the warmth of their love and support washing over him, a comforting reminder of the foundation that had always grounded him, the unwavering belief in his potential that had fueled his ambition, his resilience, his determination to succeed.

Later that evening, after a celebratory dinner filled with laughter and shared stories, Ethan sat with his father on the porch, the cool night air a welcome contrast to the warmth of the house, the twinkling stars a silent testament to the vastness of the universe and the infinite possibilities that lay ahead.

"You know, Ethan," his father began, his voice low and thoughtful, "I've been watching you these past few months, and I've seen a change in you. You're not just growing as a professional, you're growing as a person. You're learning to navigate the complexities of the world, to balance your ambition with your values, to find your own path, your own voice."

Ethan nodded, his heart filled with gratitude for his father's wisdom, his unwavering support. "I've learned a lot, Dad. About work, about life, about myself. And I couldn't have done it without you, without Mom, without the support of my family and friends."

He paused, his gaze meeting his father's, a question forming in his mind, a question that had been lingering for weeks, a question that he finally felt ready to ask.

"Dad," he began, his voice hesitant, "how did you do it? How did you balance your career with your family, your passions, your life? How did you find fulfillment, not just success?"

His father smiled, a knowing glint in his eyes. "It's a journey, Ethan," he said, his voice filled with a lifetime of experience. "And it's not always easy. There will be challenges, setbacks, and moments of doubt. But the key is to stay true to yourself, to your values, to your dreams. Don't let the pursuit of success consume you. Don't sacrifice the things that truly matter for the sake of ambition. Find a way to integrate your work with your life, your passions with your career, your dreams with your reality."

He paused, his gaze drifting towards the starlit sky, his voice softening. "And remember, Ethan, you're not alone in this journey. You have your family, your friends, your colleagues, your mentors. Lean on them, learn from them, and let them support you. And most importantly, don't be afraid to ask for help when you need it. Vulnerability is not weakness, it's strength. It's the foundation of true connection, of genuine growth, of a life well-lived."

Ethan listened intently, his heart absorbing his father's words, his mind processing the wisdom that had been passed down through generations, the timeless truths that transcended the ever-changing landscape of the world.

He felt a surge of gratitude for his father, for his guidance, his support, his unwavering belief in him. And he felt a renewed sense of determination, a commitment to living a life that honored his values, his passions, and his dreams, a life that was both successful and fulfilling, a life that was truly his own.

**An Evening of Connection**

Later that night, Ethan found himself strolling hand-in-hand with Lauren through the moonlit park, the cool night air a welcome contrast to the warmth of their intertwined fingers. The gentle rhythm of their footsteps echoed through the quiet paths, a symphony of shared moments, of unspoken understanding, of a love that had weathered the storms and emerged stronger, more resilient, more beautiful.

They talked about their day, their dreams, their fears, their hopes for the future. They shared laughter, whispered secrets, and stolen kisses beneath the starlit sky. And as they walked, Ethan felt a sense of peace, a contentment that transcended the anxieties of the workplace, the pressures of his career, the challenges that lay ahead.

He had found his balance, his harmony, his center. He had a job that challenged him, a team that supported him, a family that loved him, and a woman who cherished him. And in that moment, as he looked into Lauren's eyes, her smile a reflection of his own happiness, he knew that he had everything he needed, everything he had ever wanted.

He was living the life he was meant to live, a life filled with purpose, passion, and connection. And he knew, with a certainty that transcended words, that the journey was just beginning.

CHAPTER XXVIII

# Bridging the Gap: A Symphony of Generations

The conference room buzzed with a nervous energy that had nothing to do with quarterly reports or sales projections. It was more like the vibe before a surprise pop quiz, except the quiz was on "How to Not Make Your Gen Z Employees Want to Quit (and Maybe Even Impress Them)." Ethan shifted in his seat, acutely aware of the eyes of SynergyWorks' leadership team fixed on him, their expressions a mixture of curiosity, skepticism, and a hint of apprehension. He tugged at his collar, the crisp button-down suddenly feeling more like a straitjacket, a symbol of the corporate conformity he'd been rebelling against since day one. Beside him, Noah sat with his usual composure, his posture straight, his hands clasped neatly in his lap, but even Ethan could detect a flicker of unease in his normally unflappable boss.

"Alright, gentlemen," began Ms. Davis, the CEO, her voice sharp and business-like, cutting through the tense silence like a knife. "We've heard a lot about this... 'intergenerational mentoring experiment' of yours. Frankly, some of us were skeptical. We thought it was just another HR initiative, a feel-good program that would fizzle out after a few weeks with no tangible results. But the results speak for themselves. The Peterson account, the data migration project – successes we haven't seen in years. These are the kind of wins that make shareholders do a happy dance, the kind of achievements that get us noticed in the industry, the kind of momentum that propels us towards a future where SynergyWorks is not just a company, but a force to be reckoned with."

She paused, her gaze sweeping across the room, her eyes settling on Ethan and Noah, a challenge in their depths. "So, spill the tea. Give us the inside scoop. What's the secret sauce that transformed a skeptical Gen Z intern and a rigid Millennial manager into a dynamic duo that's shaking up the company and delivering results that would make even Steve Jobs jealous?"

Ethan glanced at Noah, who, with a ghost of a smile, gave a subtle nod, a silent signal of encouragement and support. "Well," Ethan started, leaning forward, his voice a blend of confidence and self-deprecating humor, "it all began with a clash. A clash of styles, of perspectives, of generations. Like, imagine a penguin trying to breakdance at a rave. That was me, first day on the job, rocking a tie, a starched shirt, and a desperate need to impress. I was so extra, I probably had a LinkedIn profile before I even graduated college."

He paused, letting the image sink in, a few chuckles rippling through the room, the tension easing slightly. "When I first started here," he continued, "I saw Noah as... well, let's just say he was giving off major 'Spreadsheet Overlord' vibes. The man was practically surgically attached to his laptop, his fingers flying across the keyboard with the speed and precision of a concert pianist. The constant pressure, the obsession with deadlines, the meetings where I spent most of the time calculating the optimal mint-to-buzzword ratio – it all seemed so extra. I was like, 'Bruh, do you even know what a meme is?'"

A wave of laughter erupted, the tension in the room noticeably easing, the executives' faces softening, their curiosity piqued. Ethan grinned, his confidence growing with each chuckle, each nod of recognition. He was connecting with them, bridging the gap between his generation and theirs, using humor and relatable anecdotes to paint a picture of the challenges and opportunities that lay at the heart of the intergenerational workplace.

"Don't get me wrong, I still believe in YOLO and finding the perfect GIF for every situation," he continued, his voice a blend of sincerity and playful self-awareness. "But what I've learned from Noah is that structure and discipline aren't the enemies of innovation. They're the foundation. Without them, creativity is just chaos. And chaos doesn't deliver results. It's like trying to build a house out of emojis – it looks cool, but it's not gonna stand up in a storm."

He glanced at Noah, who was now looking at him with an expression that was almost... proud? Maybe even a little bit impressed? Ethan pressed on, his voice gaining strength, his conviction deepening. "Noah taught me the value of precision, of accountability, of following through on commitments. He showed me that success isn't just about having fire ideas, it's about executing them flawlessly, like a perfectly choreographed TikTok dance."

He paused, his gaze sweeping across the room, meeting the eyes of each executive in turn, his message resonating with a clarity and a passion that surprised even himself. "He taught me that attention to detail matters, that every data point, every connection, every validation rule – it all contributes to the bigger picture, to the success of the project, to the satisfaction of our clients. He taught me that sometimes, the most innovative solutions are born from a deep understanding of the fundamentals, from a respect for the rules, from a willingness to learn from those who have come before us."

Noah cleared his throat, taking the conversational baton, his voice surprisingly gentle, a stark contrast to the stern tone he usually employed in the office. "And Ethan," he said, his eyes twinkling with a newfound appreciation for the young man who had challenged him, inspired him, and ultimately, helped him to become a better leader, "taught me the importance of flexibility, of adaptation, of seeing the world through a different lens. He challenged my assumptions, pushed me out of my comfort zone, and reminded me that sometimes, the best solutions come from unexpected places, like a viral TikTok trend that somehow turns into a marketing goldmine."

He paused, his gaze sweeping across the expectant faces of the leadership team, his message resonating with a sincerity and a vulnerability that surprised even himself. "I used to think Gen Z was all about instant gratification, social media, and a lack of work ethic. Ethan proved me wrong. He showed me that this generation is full of passion, creativity, and a desire to make a real difference in the world. They just need the right guidance, the right support, and the right environment to thrive. They need to know that their voices matter, that their ideas are valued, that their contributions can shape the future."

He thought about the night at Riley's apartment, the music, the laughter, the shared joy of connecting on a human level, beyond the confines of their professional roles. He thought about the lessons he'd learned from Ethan, about the importance of balance, of connection, of living a life that was not just about work, but about passion, purpose, and fulfillment. And he realized that Ethan had not only helped him to become a better leader, but also a better person.

Ethan chimed back in, his voice filled with a youthful energy that resonated with the executives, reminding them of their own younger selves, their own dreams, their own aspirations. "And let's be real, sometimes that environment needs a little shaking up. We don't want beanbag chairs and ping pong tables – we want to be challenged, to be mentored, to be given the opportunity to contribute our ideas and make a real impact. We want to be part of something bigger than ourselves, something that aligns with our values and our vision for the future. We want to work hard, but we also want to live, to experience, to create, to connect. We want a work-life balance that doesn't feel like a constant battle."

He paused, his gaze meeting Ms. Davis's, a challenge and a plea in his eyes. "We want to be heard, to be respected, to be valued for our unique perspectives and contributions. We want to be part of a team, a family, a community that supports us, encourages us, and inspires us to be the best versions of ourselves."

Noah nodded in agreement. "By understanding our generational differences, by acknowledging our strengths and weaknesses, by communicating openly and honestly, we were able to build a partnership that not only benefited us personally, but also transformed our team and ultimately, the company. It's like we learned to speak each other's language, to translate the jargon, to bridge the gap between two worlds."

He looked at Ethan, a genuine smile gracing his lips, a warmth in his eyes that spoke of a deep respect and affection. "Ethan taught me that leadership isn't about control, it's about empowerment. It's about creating a space where everyone feels valued, respected, and supported. It's about fostering a culture of collaboration, where different perspectives are not just tolerated, but celebrated."

Ethan grinned back, the warmth of Noah's words filling him with a sense of gratitude and belonging. "And Noah taught me that sometimes, the best way to innovate is to first master the fundamentals. That discipline and structure are not the enemies of creativity, but the foundation upon which it can flourish. It's like learning the rules of the game before you try to change them."

Ms. Davis, who had been listening intently, her expression shifting from skepticism to curiosity to admiration, leaned forward, her voice laced with a newfound respect. "So, what you're saying is that the key to success in today's workplace is not about ignoring generational differences, but about embracing them, leveraging them, and creating a synergy that benefits everyone?"

"Exactly," Ethan and Noah said in unison, their voices echoing through the room, a testament to the harmony they had found, the partnership they had forged, the bridge they had built between two generations.

"And that," Ethan added with a final grin, "is the tea."

The room erupted in applause, the executives' faces beaming with approval, their eyes filled with a newfound understanding of the power of intergenerational collaboration, the potential for growth and innovation that lay within the diverse perspectives of their workforce. Ethan and Noah exchanged a look, a silent acknowledgment of their shared accomplishment, their journey from clashing colleagues to trusted partners, their transformation from individuals to leaders.

And as they basked in the applause, they knew that they had not only changed themselves, they had changed the company, had set in motion a cultural shift that would ripple outward, creating a more inclusive, collaborative, and fulfilling workplace for generations to come.

> "*Every Ethan needs a Noah, every Noah a Ethan and every Riley a Noah and Ethan, every Noah and Ethan, a Riley.*"

The day we realise we work with individual human beings and not structured machines, work becomes more collaborative. Thanks for reading,

Akilan A P

# Cheatsheet

**Cheat Sheet for Gen Z Employees**

1. Embrace the Grind:

- Understand that hard work and dedication are essential for success, even if it doesn't always feel glamorous or exciting.
- Don't be afraid to put in the extra effort, to go the extra mile, to show your commitment to the team and the company.
- Remember that every task, no matter how small or tedious, is an opportunity to learn, to grow, and to contribute to the bigger picture.

2. Find Your Voice:

- Don't be afraid to speak up, to share your ideas, to challenge the status quo.
- Communicate your needs, your concerns, and your aspirations clearly and respectfully.
- Advocate for your own growth and development, seek out mentors, and ask for feedback.

3. Embrace Collaboration:

- Recognize the value of teamwork, the power of diverse perspectives, and the synergy that arises when people work together towards a common goal.
- Be willing to learn from others, to share your knowledge, and to support your colleagues.
- Build relationships with your teammates, your managers, and other stakeholders, creating a network of support and collaboration.

4. Find Your Balance:

- Prioritize your well-being, your mental and physical health, your relationships, and your passions.
- Set boundaries between work and life, and don't be afraid to say no to demands that compromise your well-being.

- Remember that life is a marathon, not a sprint, and that sustainable success requires a balance between work, rest, and play.

5. Embrace Your Authenticity:

- Don't try to fit into a mold or conform to expectations that don't align with your values and aspirations.
- Be yourself, embrace your unique strengths and perspectives, and find a way to contribute your authentic self to the workplace.
- Remember that your generation has a lot to offer the world, and that your voice, your ideas, and your energy can make a real difference.

**Cheat Sheet for Managers of Gen Z**

1. Embrace the New Generation:

- Understand that Gen Z employees have a different set of values, priorities, and expectations than previous generations.
- Be open to their ideas, their perspectives, and their unique ways of working.
- Create a workplace culture that values diversity, inclusivity, and collaboration.

2. Be a Mentor, Not Just a Manager:

- Invest time in getting to know your Gen Z employees, their strengths, their weaknesses, their aspirations.
- Offer guidance, support, and encouragement, helping them to navigate the challenges of the workplace and to develop their skills and talents.
- Be a role model, demonstrating the values and behaviors you expect from your team.

3. Communicate Clearly and Effectively:

- Avoid jargon, clichés, and corporate buzzwords that can alienate and confuse Gen Z employees.
- Be direct, honest, and transparent in your communication, providing clear expectations, constructive feedback, and regular updates.
- Use a variety of communication channels to reach your team, including

in-person meetings, emails, instant messaging, and video conferencing.

4. Empower and Engage:

- Give your Gen Z employees the autonomy and responsibility they crave, allowing them to take ownership of their work and contribute their unique talents.
- Create opportunities for them to learn, to grow, and to make a real impact on the company and the world.
- Recognize and celebrate their achievements, providing positive reinforcement and fostering a sense of belonging.

5. Adapt and Evolve:

- Be willing to adapt your leadership style to meet the needs of your Gen Z employees, embracing new technologies, new ways of working, and new perspectives.
- Create a culture of continuous learning and improvement, encouraging your team to experiment, to innovate, and to challenge the status quo.
- Remember that leadership is a journey, not a destination, and that the best leaders are those who are constantly learning, growing, and evolving.

# Scorecard (gen Z Employees)

Use this scorecard to assess your workplace performance. Ask your manager to rate you across the five categories. Compare your scores to the key below and discuss areas for improvement with your manager.

| Skill/Trait | 1 (Needs Improvement) | 2 (Developing) | 3 (Proficient) | 4 (Excellent) | 5 (Exceptional) |
|---|---|---|---|---|---|
| Work Ethic | Misses deadlines, lacks focus, needs constant supervision. | Shows effort but requires guidance to stay on track. | Meets deadlines, produces good work, shows initiative. | Exceeds expectations, takes ownership, proactive. | Sets a high standard, inspires others, consistently delivers outstanding results. |
| Communication | Struggles to express ideas clearly, avoids difficult conversations. | Communicates effectively in casual settings, needs to develop professional skills. | Communicates clearly and respectfully, actively listens. | Communicates with confidence, builds rapport, conveys complex information. | Masterfully communicates, inspires, builds strong relationships. |
| Collaboration | Struggles to work with others, avoids team projects. | Participates in team projects but needs guidance. | Works well with others, contributes to discussions, shares ideas. | Actively collaborates, fosters positive environment, resolves conflicts. | Excels at teamwork, inspires collaboration, contributes to team success. |
| Adaptability | Resists change, struggles to adapt, prefers routine. | Adapts with effort, needs time to adjust. | Adapts readily, embraces challenges, demonstrates flexibility. | Thrives in dynamic environments, seeks new experiences, adapts quickly. | Excels at navigating change, inspires others to adapt, consistently demonstrates resilience. |
| Problem-Solving | Struggles to identify and solve problems, relies on others. | Approaches problems with basic understanding, needs guidance. | Effectively identifies and solves problems, applies critical thinking. | Proactively identifies and solves complex problems, develops innovative solutions. | Excels at problem-solvin g, inspires critical thinking, delivers exceptional solutions. |

For Gen Z Employees

**Overall Score:**

4-5: You're a workplace rockstar! You consistently exceed expectations, demonstrating a strong work ethic, exceptional communication skills, and a collaborative spirit. You're proactive, adaptable, and a true problem-solver.

Keep shining and inspiring those around you!

3-4: You're on the right track and making steady progress! You're meeting expectations and demonstrating growth in key areas. Continue to hone your skills, build strong relationships with your colleagues, and find a healthy balance between your work and personal life. You have a bright future ahead of you!

2-3: You're making progress, but there's room for improvement. You're meeting some expectations but may need to focus on specific areas to enhance your performance. Identify your weaknesses, seek feedback from your manager and mentors, and actively work on developing your skills and confidence.

1-2: You're facing some challenges in adapting to the workplace. This is a new environment with new expectations, and it's okay to need some extra support. Reach out to your manager, mentors, and colleagues for guidance. Focus on developing your skills, understanding the nuances of the work environment, and building a strong foundation for success.

# Scorecard (gen Z Managers)

Use this scorecard to assess your workplace performance. Ask your Gen Z employees to rate you across the five categories. Compare your scores to the key below and discuss areas for improvement with your Gen Z team.

| Skill/Trait | 1 (Needs Improvement) | 2 (Developing) | 3 (Proficient) | 4 (Excellent) | 5 (Exceptional) |
|---|---|---|---|---|---|
| Understanding Gen Z | Relies on stereotypes, struggles to connect. | Shows some understanding, but needs to deepen knowledge. | Understands key values and motivations, adapts communication. | Demonstrates empathy and insights, builds strong relationships. | Deeply understands and appreciates Gen Z, creates a supportive workplace. |
| Mentorship | Provides limited guidance, focuses on tasks. | Offers some support, needs to develop mentoring skills. | Provides regular guidance and feedback, supports growth. | Creates a culture of mentorship, empowers employees. | Inspires and motivates through exceptional mentorship, fosters learning. |
| Communication | Relies on jargon, struggles to be clear. | Adapts communication somewhat, but needs improvement. | Communicates clearly, avoids jargon, actively listens. | Communicates effectively, builds trust. | Masterfully communicates, inspires, fosters dialogue. |
| Empowerment | Micromanages, limits autonomy, stifles creativity. | Delegates some tasks, but needs to provide more autonomy. | Empowers ownership, encourages initiative. | Creates a culture of empowerment, fosters collaboration. | Inspires employees to reach their potential, creates a valued workplace. |
| Adaptability | Resistant to change, struggles to adapt to new ways of working. | Adapts with effort, needs to embrace change more readily. | Adapts to new technologies and styles, embraces innovation. | Champions change, encourages experimentatio n, fosters growth mindset. | Leads in adapting to the evolving workplace, inspires others to embrace change. |

For Gen Z Managers

**Overall Score:**

4-5: You're a natural! You possess an exceptional understanding of Gen Z and have mastered the art of creating a thriving environment where they can flourish. Your mentorship skills are top-notch, and you communicate with clarity and empathy, empowering your Gen Z team members to reach their full potential. You readily adapt to the evolving needs of the modern workplace and champion change and innovation. Keep up the fantastic work!

3-4: You're on the right path! You have a good grasp of Gen Z's values and motivations and are developing strong mentorship and communication skills. You're making progress in empowering your team and adapting to new ways of working. Continue to build relationships, refine your approach, and embrace the unique perspectives of your Gen Z employees.

2-3: You're making progress, but there's room to grow! While you're beginning to understand Gen Z, you may need to delve deeper into their perspectives and refine your communication and mentorship skills. Focus on empowering your team and adapting to the changing workplace dynamics to better support your Gen Z employees.

1-2: You're facing some challenges! The traditional workplace approach may not be effective in leading and motivating Gen Z. It's time to seek out resources, engage in open conversations with your Gen Z team members, and actively learn from their perspectives and experiences. Embrace new ways of working, adapt your communication style, and focus on building trust and rapport with your Gen Z employees.

www.ingramcontent.com/pod-product-compliance
Lightning Source LLC
LaVergne TN
LVHW041218150826
845673LV00001B/448

*9798897243815*